THE USBORNE
INTERNET - LINKED
ENCYCLOPEDIA OF
ANCIENT
EGYPT

Gill Harvey
and Struan Reid

Designed by Linda Penny and Melissa Alaverdy

Illustrated by Inklink Firenze, Ian Jackson and Aziz Khan

Edited by Jane Chisholm

Consultant: Dr Anne Millard

Cover design: Stephen Wright and Zöe Wray
Additional design: Sarah Cronin and Andrea Slane
Digital imaging: John Russell

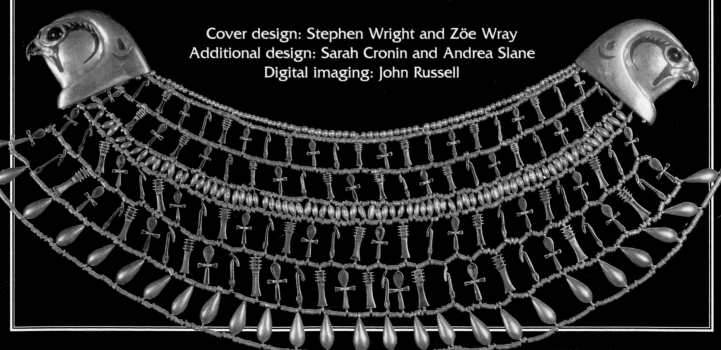

INTERNET SAFETY

When using the Internet, please make sure you follow these guidelines:

- Ask for your parent or guardian's permission before you connect to the Internet.

- If you write a message in a Web site guest book or on a Web site message board, do not include any personal information, such as your full name, address or telephone number, and ask an adult before you give your e-mail address.

- If a Web site asks you to log in or register by typing your name or e-mail address, ask an adult for permission first.

- If you do receive e-mail from someone you don't know, tell an adult and do not reply to the e-mail.

- Never arrange to meet someone you have talked to on the Internet.

All the sites described in this book have been selected by Usborne editors as suitable, in their opinion, for children, although no guarantees can be given and Usborne Publishing is not responsible for the accuracy or suitability of the information on any Web site other than its own. We recommend that young children are supervised while on the Internet, and that children do not use Internet Chat Rooms.

SITE AVAILABILITY

The links in Usborne Quicklinks are regularly reviewed and updated, but occasionally you may get a message saying that a site is unavailable. This might be temporary, so try again later. If any of the recommended sites close down, we will, if possible, replace them with suitable alternatives, so you will always find an up-to-date list of sites.

WHAT YOU NEED

All the Web sites listed in this book can be accessed with a standard home computer and an Internet browser (this is the software that enables your computer to display information from the Internet). Here is a list of basic requirements:

- a PC with Microsoft® Windows® 98 or later version, or a Macintosh computer with System 9.0, or later version

- 64Mb RAM

- a browser such as Microsoft® Internet Explorer 5, or Netscape® 4.7, or later versions

- connection to the Internet via a modem (preferably 56Kbps) or a faster digital or cable line

- an account with an Internet Service Provider (ISP)

- a sound card to hear sound files

EXTRAS

Some Web sites need additional programs, called plug-ins, to play sound files or show videos, animations or 3-D images. If you go to a site but do not have the necessary plug-in, a message should appear on the screen.

There is usually a button on the site that you can click on to download a plug-in, or go to **www.usborne-quicklinks. com** and click on 'Net Help'. Here are some plug-ins you might need:

QUICKTIME – lets you view videos. This is a trademark of Apple computer, Inc., registered in the US and other countries.

REALPLAYER® – lets you play videos and hear sound files. This is a trademark of RealNetworks, Inc., registered in the US and other countries.

SHOCKWAVE® – enables you to play animations and interactive programs. This is a trademark of Macromedia, Inc., registered in the US and other countries.

COMPUTER VIRUSES

A computer virus is a small program that can seriously damage your computer. A virus can get into your computer when you download programs from the Internet, or in an attachment that arrives with an e-mail.

You can buy anti-virus software at computer stores, or download it from the Internet. To find out more about viruses, go to **www.usborne-quicklinks.com** and click on 'Net Help'.

DISCOVERING ANCIENT EGYPT

The ancient Egyptian civilization began to wane in 30BC, when Egypt became part of the Roman Empire. Christianity took over, and the treasures that lay buried in the desert were gradually forgotten. Then, about 200 years ago, European explorers started taking an interest in the ancient sites. For some, this soon became an obsession.

EARLY RECORDS

The ancient Egyptians wrote a lot down, but they wrote to glorify their gods and king, not to create accurate records. So they deliberately left some things out and exaggerated others. The first real history of Egypt was written by a Greek, named Herodotus, who is sometimes known as the Father of History. He visited Egypt in around 500BC. His account was mainly based on what people told him, so some of it was myth rather than fact.

Herodotus

Later, in the Ptolemaic period (see page 37), Ptolemy II paid an Egyptian scribe named Manetho to write a history of Egypt. Manetho divided it into 30 dynasties, or groups of kings, a system we still use today.

The Pyramids of Giza, which have amazed visitors for thousands of years.

This is the Rosetta Stone. Although the French found it, the British claimed it when they defeated Napoleon off the coast of Egypt. It is still in the British Museum in London.

THE VITAL CLUE

For European explorers in the 18th century, it was difficult to make sense of the ancient monuments. They couldn't tell who had built them, when or why, because they couldn't read hieroglyphs, the Egyptian picture writing.

Then, in 1798, Britain and France went to war, and fought in Egypt. Napoleon, the French general, took a big team of scholars with him to study the monuments. But it was his soldiers who made the most important discovery – a slab of black stone, near the Mediterranean sea, at a place called Rosetta. It had three different scripts on it – one Greek, and two Egyptian. The French scholars guessed that the texts were translations of each other. Could this be the key to the mysterious hieroglyphs?

THE BIRTH OF EGYPTOLOGY

The Rosetta Stone, as it became known, did indeed make it possible to decipher hieroglyphs. Most of the work was done by a Frenchman, Jean-François Champollion, and an Englishman, Thomas Young. Once people could read hieroglyphs, interest in ancient Egypt shot up, and a new academic subject was created: Egyptology.

BELZONI THE GIANT

Excitement about Egypt's treasures led to what we now think of as reckless plundering. Adventurers thought it fine to ransack tombs and temples, taking whatever they fancied. One was the ex circus strongman Giovanni Belzoni, who was over 2m (6' 7") tall. He cleared the sand from the big temples at Abu Simbel, and opened many of the kings' tombs in the Valley of the Kings. In his enthusiasm, he caused a lot of damage – but in fact, he was no worse than other adventurers of his time.

A French coin commemorating Jean-François Champollion's work on hieroglyphs

AUGUSTE MARIETTE

By the mid-19th century, Egypt was attracting more and more enthusiasts. One was a Frenchman named Auguste Mariette. Without permission from the authorities, he began to dig at Saqqara, and soon found a huge underground tomb that became known as the Serapeum.

This was the start of Mariette's great career as an Egyptologist. As well as carrying out many excavations, he set up the Egyptian Museum in Cairo. This meant that most new discoveries stayed in Egypt, where they belonged, rather than being shipped out to European countries.

THE MAN IN PINK UNDERWEAR

Mariette was not as reckless as Belzoni, but even so, careful methods of excavation were only developed later in the 19th century. This was thanks to an eccentric Englishman – William Flinders Petrie. He often worked in just his long, pink underwear to stay cool.

Petrie created a very detailed and disciplined way of working. He saw that as much could be learned from small objects and fragments of pottery as from big monuments. He recorded everything he found and, by comparing thousands of pots with each other, he began to sort out the mystery surrounding Egypt's earliest history.

Flinders Petrie, whose work is still highly respected by Egyptologists today

Belzoni's men hauling off a statue from Luxor, to be transported to England

TREASURE TROVE

By the early 20th century, many Egyptologists had followed in Belzoni's path, hunting for mummies and treasure in the Valley of the Kings. All the tombs they found had been robbed in ancient times, and almost everyone was convinced that there was nothing left to discover. But one man didn't agree...

One of Tutankhamun's necklaces, inlaid with jewels

THE MISSING TOMB

Egyptologists had established which kings had been buried in the Valley of the Kings. All the important ones had been found, but one was still missing: the boy king Tutankhamun (see page 28). A British Egyptologist named Howard Carter was determined to find him. In 1917 he started to hunt, funded by a wealthy man, Lord Carnarvon. For four years he found nothing, and the Egyptian authorities thought it was time he gave up. But Carter begged for one more year. Eventually, they agreed.

WONDERFUL THINGS

The hunt restarted in November 1922. Carter decided to move some ancient workmen's huts – and almost as soon as work began, some steps appeared, leading down to a tomb. Could this be it – success at last? Very excited, Carter sent Lord Carnarvon a telegram saying, *At last have made wonderful discovery in Valley. A magnificent tomb with seals intact. Recovered same for your arrival. Congratulations.* On November 25th 1922, Lord Carnarvon stood waiting while Howard Carter carefully made a hole in the blocked-up door... and looked inside. Impatiently, Lord Carnarvon called, "Can you see anything?" And Howard Carter replied, "Yes, wonderful things."

Howard Carter beginning the long, careful job of cleaning Tutankhamun's coffins

A TEST OF PATIENCE

The first room was full of objects heaped together, such as chariots, statues, chairs and chests. At one end was another sealed door with two statues guarding it. Could the mummy of the king lie behind it? Even though everyone was dying to know, Carter was patient. First, he cleared the first room, taking detailed records of everything. At last, in February 1923, he opened the second door. What he found inside was breathtaking – four wooden shrines, covered in gold, surrounding a solid stone sarcophagus. Beyond was yet another room packed with more amazing objects. But Carter continued to be incredibly patient. It was another three years before he opened the sarcophagus to find three coffins, nestled

This pendant, shaped like a scarab, is inlaid with lapis, carnelian and turquoise.

inside each other. The first two were made of gilded wood, but the third was solid gold, inlaid with precious stones. Inside lay the mummy, its face covered with the beautiful gold mask that is now recognized all over the world.

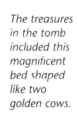

The treasures in the tomb included this magnificent bed shaped like two golden cows.

THE MUMMY'S CURSE?

Not long after the discovery of the tomb, Lord Carnarvon developed pneumonia. He died in Cairo on April 5th 1923. Sadly, this meant that he never saw Tutankhamun's stunning gold coffin or mask, because the sarcophagus had yet to be opened. Some newspaper reporters suggested that he had died under a curse, which doomed anyone who disturbed the mummy. People wanted to believe the story, so it spread quickly. But most people who had contact with the mummy, including Carter himself, came to no harm at all.

Tutankhamun's famous mask had yet to be uncovered when Lord Carnarvon died.

INTERNET LINK

At **www.usborne-quicklinks.com** *you'll find a link to the* **National Geographic Web site**, *where you can read an eyewitness's account of viewing Tutankhamun's tomb in 1923.*

RECORDS AND CONSERVATION

Egyptology isn't just about finding new things. Many tombs, buildings and objects have been found that risk being lost forever unless they are recorded and preserved properly. The work can range from making an intricate copy of a small carving to actually moving whole buildings. Many Egyptologists now believe that this is much more urgent than carrying out new excavations.

A stonemason working with restorers at Saqqara

19TH-CENTURY RECORDS

This painting by the 19th-century painter David Roberts shows the temples of Ramesses II at Abu Simbel almost covered in sand.

Making records may not seem as exciting as excavating. But if more of the early explorers had recorded their finds properly, many of the remaining mysteries might have been solved. Even early in the 19th century, though, some records were made. David Roberts, a Scottish painter, made a series of careful oil paintings, and a German named Karl Lepsius carried out a detailed survey of all the major sites.

MODERN DISCIPLINES

As well as excavators, the world of Egyptology includes people who specialize in examining, reconstructing and recording objects such as pots, coffins or ancient writings; mappers, who make plans of ancient sites; restorers, who specialize in preserving fragile paintings or objects; photographers, who provide clear and accurate records; and scientists of many kinds who use modern technology to examine and date objects.

SAVED FROM BEETLES

Not all conservation takes place in Egypt. In 1976, the Egyptian authorities sent a major exhibition of antiquities to Paris. The key exhibit was the mummy of Ramesses II, which was given its own special passport to enter France. When it was found that Ramesses was being attacked by beetles, French scientists offered to help, and the king was treated successfully.

The mummy of Ramesses II, now back in Cairo

🪶 INTERNET LINK

*At **www.usborne-quicklinks.com** you'll find a link to an interesting Web site, where you can read about the history of the conservation of the Sphinx, and the ongoing difficulties of preserving this ancient monument.*

DESERT RESCUE

In the 1960s, one of the world's greatest ever conservation projects took place in Nubia (southern Egypt). To control the Nile's water so that crops could be grown all year, a big dam was built, creating a huge reservoir. This would have flooded all the ancient sites in the area, including the temples at Abu Simbel.

The Egyptian government wanted to rescue as much as possible, but the only solution for the temples was to move them. This was too expensive for one government, so UNESCO (United Nations Educational, Scientific and Cultural Organization) helped. Money flooded in, and the amazing task of moving the temples began in 1964. Over four years, the temples were cut into blocks and moved 60m (197ft) up the cliff face, out of the way of the water.

THE JOB GOES ON

Preserving ancient Egyptian sites is a difficult job. Ones that are open to tourists can easily be damaged – by the moisture in people's breath, for example – and there often isn't enough time or money to preserve the many others. But a great deal of work is still done by the Egyptian Supreme Council of Antiquities and by Egyptologists from around the world.

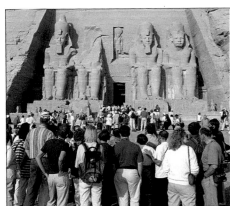

Abu Simbel is now a major tourist site.

Ramesses' temple was cut into 1,036 pieces, each weighing between 7 and 30 tonnes (tons).

Restoration experts worked on the blocks of stone to disguise the seams.

EGYPTOLOGY TODAY

Egyptologists are as busy as ever. They don't expect to find another tomb like Tutankhamun's, but they are always finding vital new information about life in ancient Egypt. As technology develops, new interpretations of the facts become possible, too.

WHAT'S GOING ON?

The Egyptologists' 'season' is generally from autumn to spring, when it's not too hot. Then, Egyptologists of many nationalities work on all sorts of projects. A good way to find out about them is on the Internet. Many do not set out to find new treasures, but to record existing discoveries, or to develop a new theory about why things happened the way they did. Much of the work that goes on is restoration work (see pages 10-11). A recent successful restoration project has been that of the beautiful tomb of Nefertari on the west bank at Luxor, which was being damaged by salty water rising up beneath it.

A restorer works on the wooden model of an official, found near the pyramids of Saqqara in 1999.

Excavations are still ongoing at Saqqara. This picture shows an excavation team at the site of a newly discovered tomb in 2001.

MODERN TECHNOLOGY

Advances in technology have made a big difference to the analysis of Egyptologists' finds. CAT scanners allow them to look at mummies without damaging them, and DNA testing tells us a lot about how people were related, or what diseases they had (see page 63). Computers help Egyptologists to piece together what ruined buildings must have looked like, even when they only have fragments to work with.

 INTERNET LINKS

*At **www.usborne-quicklinks.com** you'll find a link to the **Egyptian Supreme Council of Antiquities Web site**, which has interesting links and articles as well as details of ongoing digs. You'll also find a link to the **Egypt Exploration Society Web site**, which has a 'digging diary' of all Egypt Exploration Society excavations. For a broader view of what's going on in Egyptology, follow the link to the **Egyptology Resources Web site**. As well as lots of links to interesting sites and ongoing excavations, you can find out about becoming an Egyptologist.*

A DONKEY'S DISCOVERY

One day in 1997, out in the Western Desert at a place called el Bawati, a donkey trapped his leg in a hole in the ground and fell. His rider realised that the hole might be important, and in March 1999 a major excavation began. The finds have been astonishing – a vast tomb complex containing hundreds of mummies. This is now known as 'The Valley of the Golden Mummies'.

The mummies are mostly in very good condition, and are dated from the Greek period onwards (see page 37). Some are in coffins, while others are simply wrapped in linen; many are richly decorated with gold and other metals.

The face of a golden mummy stares up from its uncovered tomb at el Bawati.

UNDER THE WAVES

Modern sonar and diving equipment open up many possibilities for underwater excavation. Divers working in the bay of Aboukir, near Alexandria, have made some very exciting discoveries in the past few years – including a palace that may have belonged to Cleopatra VII herself. Then, in June 2000, two lost, sunken cities called Herakleion and Canopus were found as well. Work continues to uncover the bay's secrets from underneath many thick layers of silt.

ONGOING WORK

These are some of the most significant discoveries and projects that have happened in Egypt over the last ten years. Much of the work is still going on.

- Pyramid workers' bakeries and temples have been found at Giza
- Some of the earliest writing in the world has been found at Abydos, and also some 1st dynasty ships
- Another tomb, KV 5, has been rediscovered in the Valley of the Kings
- The ancient city of Memphis is gradually being excavated
- A workmen's village has been uncovered at Tell el Amarna (Akhenaten's ancient capital)
- A hunt is ongoing in the Valley of the Kings for members of Akhenaten's family
- Hatshepsut's temple at Deir el Bahri is gradually being pieced back together.

One of the divers in Aboukir Bay comes face to face with an ancient sphinx.

MAP OF ANCIENT EGYPT

ANATOLIA

Carchemish •

R. Euphrates

SYRIA

CRETE

Kadesh

CYPRUS

Byblos •

LEBANON

MEDITERRANEAN SEA

• Megiddo

Jerusalem •

PALESTINE

Rosetta

Alexandria •

Tanis

Sais •

Avaris
(Per Ramesses)

This map shows the Nile Valley and the area to the north-east, now known as the Near or Middle East.

• Siwa

Giza •

WESTERN DESERT

FAIYUM

Memphis •

SINAI

Place names change over time, so more recent ones are shown in brackets.

E G Y P T

R. Nile

• Beni Hasan

Hermopolis •

Below is a more detailed map of the Nile Delta.

Akhetaten (Amarna)

EASTERN DESERT

RED SEA

Abydos •

Dendera •

Thebes (Luxor)

Esna •

Edfu •

Kom Ombo •

Aswan •

Abu Simbel

NUBIA

THE NILE DELTA

Rosetta •

Buto •

Alexandria •

Sais •

Tanis •

Avaris •

Bubastis •

Giza •

Heliopolis •

Abusir •

Saqqara •

Memphis •

Dahshur •

FAIYUM

Meidum •

14

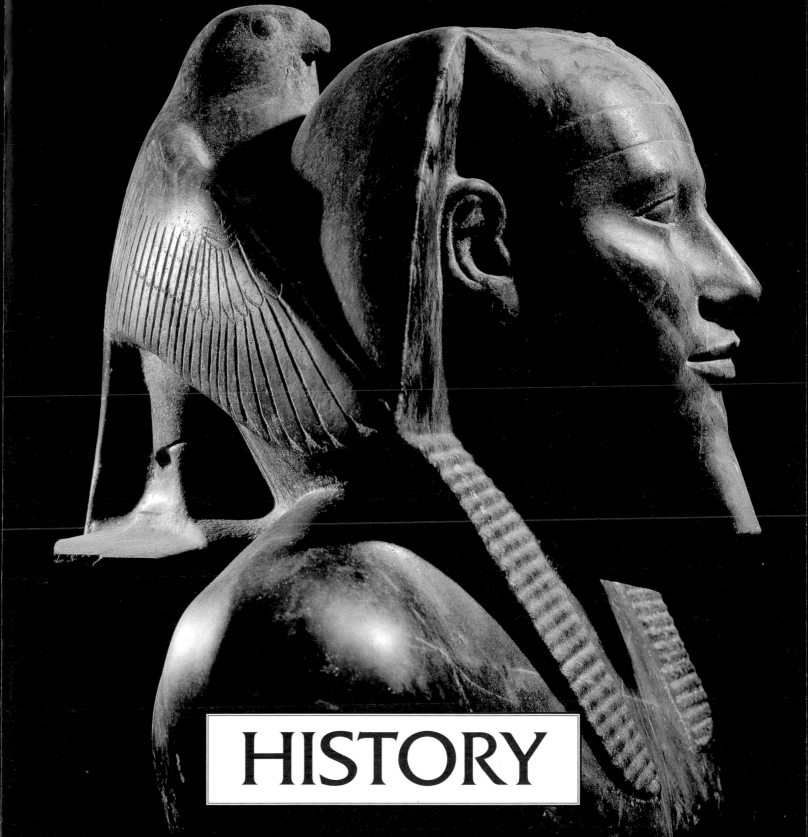

HISTORY

EARLY EGYPT

The river Nile, snaking its way across the desert and into the sea, first attracted people to its banks many thousands of years ago. At first, they moved around and survived by hunting animals and gathering what they could to eat. Then, by around 5500BC, people started to settle along the riverbank and grow crops.

THE PREDYNASTIC PERIOD

Until around 3500BC, things changed slowly. This time is called the Predynastic Period. People farmed the land along the Nile, and began to dig irrigation canals to make more use of its water. They kept animals, too – mainly sheep, goats and pigs.

There were two main groups of villages – one in the south (Upper Egypt), and one in the north (Lower Egypt). These areas gradually became two kingdoms (which means they were ruled by kings). In Upper Egypt, early mud-brick tombs or 'mastabas' have been found that contain beautiful pots and objects. These suggest that a sophisticated culture and religion were already developing, and a belief in life after death.

This Predynastic pot is decorated with a crocodile, common in the Nile at that time.

This Predynastic terracotta dancing woman is nearly 6,000 years old.

These are copies of carved ivory labels found at Abydos – examples of some of the earliest writing in the world.

WRITING BEGINS

It's likely that writing began in Egypt earlier than anywhere else in the world. We know this because of some carvings, dating from Predynastic times, that were recently found at Abydos (a town in central Egypt). The Egyptian language was written in pictures or hieroglyphs. Find out more about this on pages 86-87.

TWO CROWNS

The kings of Upper and Lower Egypt had their own separate gods and crowns. The southern king was guarded by the vulture goddess Nekhmet, and wore a tall white crown. In Lower Egypt, the king wore a red crown and was protected by the cobra goddess Wadjet.

White crown of Upper Egypt

Red crown of Lower Egypt

Later kings sometimes combined the red and white crowns to make a single crown, like this.

FIRST KING – OR KINGS?

Around 3100BC, it seems that Upper Egypt defeated Lower Egypt in a battle, and the two areas were united for the first time. The man who then became king is a slightly mysterious figure, because three different names appear in records: Menes, Narmer and Hor-Aha. This could be because kings always had more than one name. It's also possible that Hor-Aha was Narmer's son. Whatever the truth is, the Narmer palette (see below) is one of the earliest records of a king who ruled both Upper and Lower Egypt.

The Narmer palette shows King Narmer wearing the white crown of Upper Egypt. On the other side of the palette, he is shown wearing the red crown of Lower Egypt.

THE ARCHAIC PERIOD

Once Egypt was united, the land was ruled by kings for more than 3,000 years. The 1st and 2nd dynasties form the Archaic period, which lasted about 400 years. Menes (or Narmer) created a capital city for the whole country between Upper and Lower Egypt, at the bottom of the Nile Delta. This was called Memphis, which became a great city with its own special god called Ptah.

The god Ptah

Archaic mastabas, like this one at Saqqara, were made of mud brick, then painted.

FUNERAL CUSTOMS

Some of the remaining features of the Archaic period are rectangular mastabas, which were the burial places for royals and nobles. Some of the royal ones are surrounded by smaller tombs belonging to servants. It's believed that the servants would have sacrificed themselves voluntarily when their master died, and were then buried around him to see to his needs in the afterlife. This practice died out by the end of the 1st dynasty.

The Nile flows from south to north, which is why the north is called Lower Egypt and the south is called Upper Egypt. This satellite image of the river Nile shows how it meanders north from Upper Egypt then fans out into the Nile Delta.

To the east and west of the Nile there is little but harsh, scorching deserts.

THE OLD KINGDOM

The Old Kingdom was one of the most amazing periods in Egyptian history. For the first time, the Egyptians began building whole buildings in stone, with astonishing results. Many kings made sure that they would not be forgotten in a hurry, with the construction of massive monuments such as the pyramids and the Sphinx.

STABILITY AND WEALTH

The Old Kingdom began in c.2650BC with the start of the 3rd dynasty, and lasted about 500 years. At first, the king ruled all of Egypt, and sent governors to look after specific areas. They had to report back to the king on a regular basis. We now call these local governors 'nomarchs'.

This stable situation was disrupted after the reign of Pepi II. Pepi reigned for so long that he didn't have any successors, and different nomarchs took over instead.

THE FIRST GENIUS

The second king of the 3rd dynasty was called Djoser. He is famous because the first ever step pyramid was built for him, thanks to the ideas of an architect called Imhotep. Imhotep was the first recorded genius – as well as being an architect, he was a priest, a doctor, an astronomer and a very wise adviser. He was so admired by ancient Egyptians that, many years after his death, he was worshipped as a god.

A small carving of the architect Imhotep

SENEFERU

The idea of building a pyramid to rest in after death appealed to many kings after Djoser. The first king of the 4th dynasty, Seneferu, built two pyramids at Dahshur. These are known as the Bent Pyramid, and the Red Pyramid (the first true pyramid). King Seneferu was probably buried in the Red Pyramid.

Mastaba

Step pyramid

Bent pyramid

True pyramid

Djoser's step pyramid at Saqqara began as just a stone mastaba, and the steps were gradually built up.

INTERNET LINK

Go to **www.usborne-quicklinks.com** for a link to **PBS Nova Web site**, where you can find fascinating facts and figures about the pyramids, and explore inside the Great Pyramid.

GIZA

Seneferu's son, Khufu (also known by his Greek name of Cheops), built only one pyramid, but it was the most impressive ever built: the Great Pyramid of Giza. When Khufu died, his son Khafre (Chephren) built another huge pyramid next to his father's. No one matched Khufu's effort, though, and the third pyramid of Giza, built by Khafre's son Menkaure (Mycerinus), is smaller than Khafre's. You can find out more about these three amazing pyramids on pages 66-67.

This tiny carving is the only surviving image of Khufu to have been found.

A DOTTED DESERT

In the 5th and 6th dynasties, kings continued to build pyramids – there are about 90 of them dotted over the west bank of the Nile.

However, later kings didn't put as much time and effort into building them, so they didn't last as well. Most of them are now just piles of rubble.

This picture is of the pyramid of Teti at Saqqara, which now lies in ruins.

THE LAST KING

The last king of the 6th Dynasty was called Pepi II. He reigned for a long time, probably until he was about 100. After his death, Egypt fell into a period of confusion as the nomarchs vied for power, and the Old Kingdom came to an end.

THE RIDDLE OF THE SPHINX

The Sphinx sits in front of Khafre's pyramid at Giza, and has a lion's body and the head of a king. Most historians think it was built at around the same time as the pyramid, and is a portrait of Khafre himself.

The Sphinx has always captured people's imagination. Some people still think it has mysterious powers, or that there are undiscovered chambers deep inside it. But, so far, tests carried out by Egyptologists have found no evidence for anything like this.

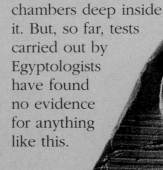

The Sphinx stares out towards the rising sun. Its front paws have recently been restored.

TIMES OF CHANGE

When the Old Kingdom dissolved, a time known as the First Intermediate Period began. Texts speak of '70 kings in 70 days' because kings came and went like the wind. Then, after about a hundred years, the Middle Kingdom began. This lasted for about 400 years, and was a period of great creativity in Egypt.

Map showing location of Middle Kingdom capital

Memphis •

It-tawy •

Faiyum

Nile

Fertile area

CHAOS AND FAMINE

Nomarchs formed the 7th, 8th, 9th and 10th dynasties. During the 9th and 10th dynasties, some of them were very powerful, but no king ruled all of Egypt. It was a period of struggle and civil war. There were also terrible famines. Low annual floods led to droughts in which crops failed and people began to starve.

Mentuhotep II

ORDER AT LAST

After about a hundred years, things improved. The princes of Thebes won control of all Egypt and made Thebes the capital for the first time. This marks the start of the 11th dynasty and the Middle Kingdom. The best known of the 11th dynasty kings, Mentuhotep II, built a magnificent mortuary temple and tomb on the west bank of the Nile, opposite Thebes.

A MYSTERY CAPITAL

Although the Middle Kingdom kings were from Thebes, in the 12th dynasty they moved their capital to a place further north. They called it It-tawy, which means 'Seizer of the Two Lands'.

No one is sure exactly where It-tawy was, but it was somewhere between Memphis and the Faiyum, a huge oasis with a lake forming part of it. One 12th dynasty king, Senusret II, started a massive irrigation project there, so that the land around it could be used for farming.

These models are of Middle Kingdom fishermen, who would have mingled with people enjoying themselves on the river.

 INTERNET LINK

At **www.usborne-quicklinks.com** you'll find a link to a Web site where you can read an article about the discovery and excavation of the Middle Kingdom town of Kahun, near the Faiyum.

CONQUERING NUBIA

The Middle Kingdom was a relatively peaceful time, but the kings of the 12th dynasty did expand Egypt southwards and conquered much of Nubia and Kush (part of modern Sudan). To guard their new territory, they built massive forts along the borders.

CREATIVE TIMES

Artistic activity flourished in the Middle Kingdom. Many famous stories were written, such as *The Tale of Sinuhe* and *The Eloquent Peasant*. These were copied over and over again by scribes in future generations, which is why we know about them today.

The model fishermen date from c.2000BC, and were found in the tomb of a man called Meket-Re in Thebes.

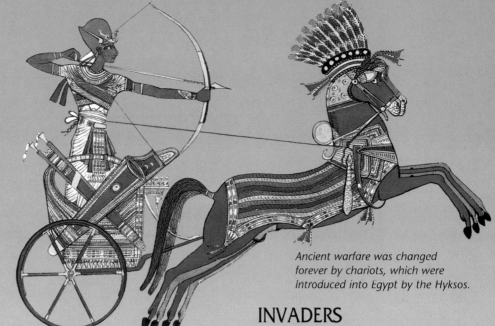

Ancient warfare was changed forever by chariots, which were introduced into Egypt by the Hyksos.

Burial practices changed, too, which led to the development of new art forms. Nobles were buried in beautifully decorated tombs cut into the rocks. Those who couldn't afford lavish decoration in their tombs had little models placed in them instead, many of them incredibly detailed and intricate. Some of the best examples were found in central Egypt, at Beni Hasan and Assyut.

INVADERS

After the 13th dynasty, royal power grew weaker and the Middle Kingdom came to an end. Meanwhile, foreigners trickled into the Nile Delta area from the east. The Egyptians called them Hyksos. The Hyksos adapted well to life in Egypt, taking on its customs and religion. They gradually became more powerful until they controlled most of Egypt from their capital, Avaris. They had a big impact on Egyptian life, and introduced many new objects, including weapons.

THE GROWTH OF EMPIRES

The Hyksos kings were hated by Egyptian princes further south. Once more, it was rulers from Thebes who became powerful enough to act. Three Theban kings – Tao I, Kamose and Ahmose – campaigned northwards and drove the Hyksos right out of Egypt. By 1550BC, a new era of Egyptian history had begun.

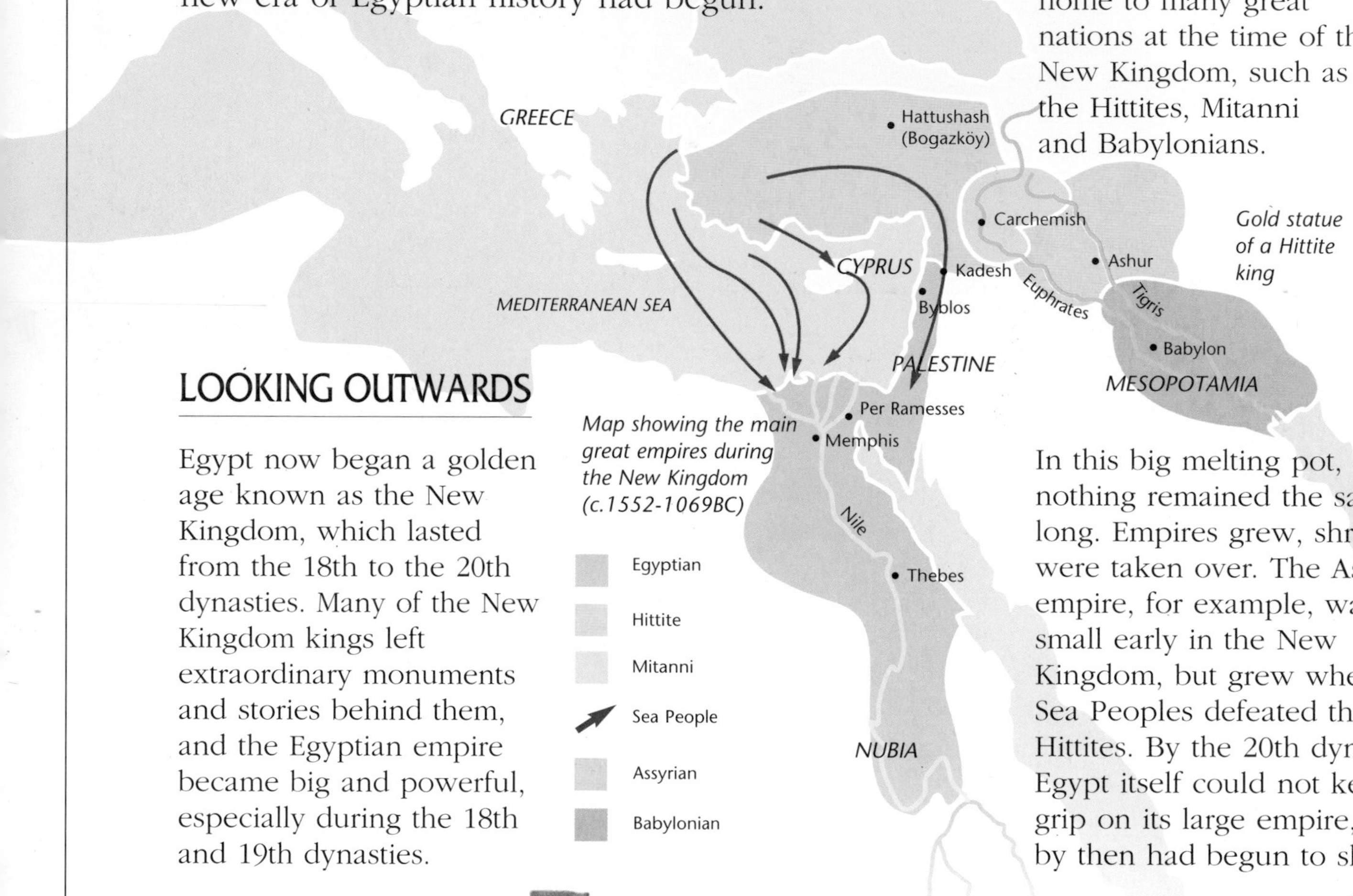

EGYPT'S MAIN RIVALS

The Near East is the term used for the countries to the north and east of Egypt as far as modern-day Turkey and Iraq. This big area was the home to many great nations at the time of the New Kingdom, such as the Hittites, Mitanni and Babylonians.

Gold statue of a Hittite king

LOOKING OUTWARDS

Egypt now began a golden age known as the New Kingdom, which lasted from the 18th to the 20th dynasties. Many of the New Kingdom kings left extraordinary monuments and stories behind them, and the Egyptian empire became big and powerful, especially during the 18th and 19th dynasties.

Map showing the main great empires during the New Kingdom (c.1552-1069BC)

- Egyptian
- Hittite
- Mitanni
- → Sea People
- Assyrian
- Babylonian

In this big melting pot, nothing remained the same for long. Empires grew, shrank, or were taken over. The Assyrian empire, for example, was small early in the New Kingdom, but grew when the Sea Peoples defeated the Hittites. By the 20th dynasty, Egypt itself could not keep a grip on its large empire, which by then had begun to shrink.

Map labels: GREECE, Hattushash (Bogazköy), Carchemish, Ashur, CYPRUS, Kadesh, Euphrates, Tigris, MEDITERRANEAN SEA, Byblos, Babylon, PALESTINE, MESOPOTAMIA, Per Ramesses, Memphis, Nile, Thebes, NUBIA

WEALTH AND GRANDEUR

Having a big empire made Egypt very wealthy, because it received a constant supply of goods from the nations it had conquered. Being powerful made trading easier, too. Egypt exported food, and imported horses, timber, metal and many other treasures.

At home, the kings revelled in their power and wealth by carrying out huge building projects. One of the most outstanding was the temple complex at Karnak. There had been temples on this site since the Middle Kingdom, but New Kingdom rulers built around them, adding many new gates (called pylons), halls and obelisks.

The vast temple complex at Karnak as it looks today, showing the sacred lake with the remains of the temple behind it.

The New Kingdom kings lavished some of their wealth on elaborate ornaments, such as this pectoral, worn around the neck.

NEW BURIAL CUSTOMS

Now that Egypt was ruled from Thebes, the pharaohs needed a new burial site. So they started cutting magnificent tombs in a valley on the west bank, which became known as the Valley of the Kings (see pages 68-69). They also built mortuary temples on the west bank, so that they could still receive funeral offerings every day.

THE EARLY NEW KINGDOM

The first 18th dynasty kings (Ahmose, Amenhotep I and Tuthmosis I) consolidated their power by expanding the empire to the south and north, and reforming the administration. This was also a time of powerful women: Tetisheri (Ahmose's grandmother), Ahhotep I (his mother), and Ahmose Nefertari, his wife. Ahmose Nefertari acted as regent when Amenhotep I was still too young to rule himself. This paved the way for a remarkable queen in the years that followed.

Later, Ahmose Nefertari was worshipped as a goddess, as she is portrayed in this painting.

⬤ INTERNET LINK

At **www.usborne-quicklinks.com** you'll find a link to a Web site where you can take a virtual tour of the temple complex at Karnak, as well as reading more about its history.

THE QUEEN WHO BECAME KING

The 18th Dynasty had problems becoming firmly established, because the kings often died young or had sons who died before them. But Tuthmosis II, the fourth king of the dynasty, had a remarkable chief queen who took this matter into her own hands. Her name was Hatshepsut.

A BOY KING

Hatshepsut had no sons, and so her nephew, another Tuthmosis, was heir to the throne. But he was still very young when Tuthmosis II died, so Hatshepsut took over as regent. This meant keeping things under control until the new king was ready to rule.

THE REGENCY ENDS

Hatshepsut was quite a character. Being regent didn't suit her at all, and after a few years the oracle of the god Amun declared she was the true king. She was properly crowned, and began to wear all the royal regalia of a male pharaoh – even a false beard.

A statue of Hatshepsut with a beard

EXPANSION AND TRADE

During Hatshepsut's 20-year reign, she defended Egypt's frontiers in Nubia and Syria, and organized many building projects. She also renewed Egypt's trade with the land of Punt (probably Somalia). This is described on her mortuary temple. The ships had to be carried in pieces from the Nile to the Red Sea and put together again. But it was worth it for Punt's myrrh trees, frankincense, ebony, ivory, leopard skins and even baboons.

Hatshepsut's expedition to the land of Punt. Punt was rich and lush, with many trees and plants that did not grow in Egypt.

Myrrh trees were taken on board the ships with all their roots.

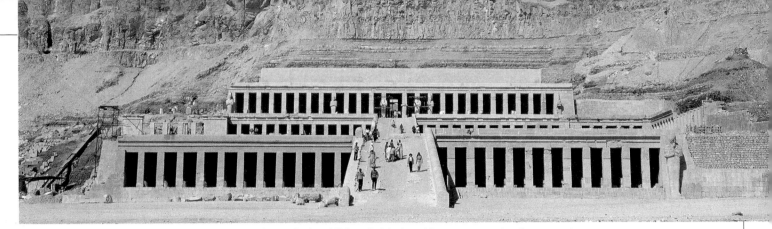

Hatshepsut's mortuary temple is a dramatic sight, with the cliff-face behind and long avenues leading up to it.

THE BEAUTIFUL TEMPLE

Hatshepsut's mortuary temple was built at Deir el Bahri, next to the temple of Mentuhotep II (see page 20). Some think it is the most beautiful of the temples still standing on the west bank of the Nile. It was designed by Hatshepsut's main adviser, a talented man named Senmut. He also educated her daughter, Neferure.

Some Egyptologists think that Senmut may have been the queen's lover. It's not clear what happened to him – he probably died in the later years of her reign, as he is no longer mentioned in records.

INTERNET LINK

At **www.usborne-quicklinks.com** you'll find a link to the **BBC History Web site**, where you can read more about the feuds, scandals and controversies surrounding Hatshepsut's reign.

THE NEPHEW'S REVENGE

Throughout Hatshepsut's reign, her nephew Tuthmosis III sat waiting in the wings, furious with her for taking his place. As soon as she was dead, he ordered everything to do with his hated aunt to be destroyed, including her temple. But now, Egyptologists are gradually rebuilding it again.

The warlike king Tuthmosis III

EGYPT AT WAR

Despite having to wait so long to become king, Tuthmosis III had a successful reign, ruling for over thirty years. He built many monuments, but he is best known for waging constant wars and extending the Egyptian empire to its greatest size ever.

The Egyptian empire at its greatest extent

SYRIA

EGYPT

Nile

RED SEA

NUBIA

Extent of Tuthmosis's empire in c.1440BC

THE MITANNI

Every spring, Tuthmosis embarked on a new military campaign, either south into Nubia or north-east into Syria, Canaan, and towards the river Euphrates. He waged a total of seventeen campaigns, many of them against a people called the Mitanni. But although he often beat them in battle, he never completely defeated them. The Mitanni were eventually destroyed by a new force from the north – the Hittites.

RELIGIOUS REVOLUTION

When Tuthmosis III died, Egypt was rich. The empire stretched far and wide, and the Mitanni made peace with his grandson, Tuthmosis IV. So Amenhotep III, who followed, was free to lead a life of luxury and concentrate on things at home. This led to a radical new approach to religion so radical that it shook the whole country.

THE POWER OF AMUN

As the New Kingdom pharaohs came from Thebes, the god of Thebes, Amun, became more and more important throughout Egypt, with rich, powerful priests. So what happened next came as a big shock.

The god Amun

A LEISURELY UPBRINGING

Amenhotep III s long, peaceful reign was ideal for spending time and resources on culture, leisure and building projects. So the heir to the throne, the young Amenhotep IV, would have had a relaxed upbringing, with plenty of freedom to develop his own ideas. He became particularly interested in religion and the arts.

This is one of many statues of Akhenaten that show him with a much longer face than other pharaohs.

INTERNET LINK

Go to www.usborne-quicklinks.com for a link to a site where you can see computer-generated reconstructions of Akhenaten's city of Akhetaten.

ONE GOD: THE ATEN

Amenhotep IV rejected the worship of Amun and replaced him with the Aten, the sun s disk in its brightest, most visible form. When he became king, he began to put his religious ideas into practice. Soon, he ordered the name Amun to be hacked off temples and told everyone to worship the Aten. He changed his name from Amenhotep to Akhenaten, which means Agreeable to the Aten .

A NEW CITY: AKHETATEN

Akhenaten didn t want to live among all the images of other gods in Thebes, so he built a new city further north and named it Akhetaten (Horizon of the Aten). It was on a windswept plain surrounded by cliffs near the area now known as Amarna, so Akhenaten s reign is often called the Amarna period.

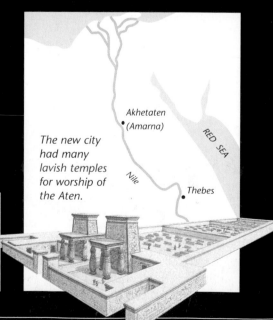

The new city had many lavish temples for worship of the Aten.

Akhetaten (Amarna)

RED SEA

Nile

Thebes

THE BEAUTIFUL QUEEN

Akhenaten s main queen was named Nefertiti, and she ruled more or less alongside him for many years. But what became of her is a mystery.

This famous bust, which experts think must be of Nefertiti, suggests she was very beautiful.

Nefertiti faded from view later on in Akhenaten s reign. It has recently been discovered that he had another queen called Kiya, who was given the title Greatly Beloved Wife . This suggests that she was very important to Akhenaten for a while. To confuse matters further, someone else seems to have been close to the king later Smenkhkare (see page 28). Smenkhkare was probably a young man, but may have been a woman.

STRANGE ART FORMS

Akhenaten encouraged a new style in the arts of sculpture and painting, especially in the first half of his reign. In his portraits, he was shown in happy family scenes, playing with his children and embracing his queen. Before this, most portraits of pharaohs were formal and idealized.

The king looked very strange in these images, with big hips, a fat, drooping belly and a long, thin face.

Akhenaten and his family worshipping the Aten. Could his strange shape have been caused by illness?

The whole family was shown with big heads and long skulls. We re still not sure why. One theory is that this style had a special religious meaning, and another is that they had some kind of illness.

THINGS CRUMBLE

Akhenaten was so busy with his religious reforms that he ignored the Hittites, new enemies to the north. This had a profound effect on Egypt s history. The Hittites started stealing provinces from the Egyptian empire, and it began to shrink. Never again did it reach the size it had been under Tuthmosis III.

THE TIMES OF TUTANKHAMUN

The reign of Akhenaten left behind a confusing situation, both for Egypt at the time and for us now. There are still many mysteries surrounding his family and descendents. Tutankhaten took over as king, aged about nine, but he relied on advisers for most of his reign, as he died when he was only nineteen.

AMARNA MYSTERIES

Akhenaten's later years are shrouded in mystery. It seems that someone named Smenkhkare ruled with him for a while. He may have taken Nefertiti's place as co-ruler; or perhaps Smenkhkare was Nefertiti herself under another name.

Although the boy king Tutankhamun didn't live long, he was buried with amazing treasures such as this gold statue.

TOMB KV55

The mystery surrounding Smenkhkare is particularly enticing because of a mummy of a man found in 1907, hastily buried in the Valley of the Kings, in a tomb labelled KV55. It was very fragile, and fell apart further when it was handled roughly. This made it difficult to establish who it was. Smenkhkare? Akhenaten? The most popular theory is that it is Akhenaten himself, but we may never know.

What's certain is that Tutankhaten came to the throne shortly after Akhenaten's death. Many now believe that he was the son of Kiya and Akhenaten. It was quite acceptable for kings to marry their sisters, and he married Ankhesenpaaten, one of Akhenaten's daughters.

This alabaster canopic jar top is thought to be of the Greatly Beloved Wife, Kiya.

THE BRIEF REIGN OF THE BOY KING

Once on the throne, Tutankhaten soon left the new city of Akhetaten and moved back to Thebes. He changed his name, from Tutankhaten ('Living image of the Aten') to Tutankhamun ('Living image of Amun'). In this way, he showed that he (or his advisers) didn't want anything more to do with Akhenaten's strange religion, and that things were going back to normal. Amun-Re was declared the principal god once more.

For much of Tutankhamun's reign, he was dependent on his older advisers. One, called Ay, was commander of chariotry for years. When Tutankhamun died without any sons, it was Ay who stepped forward to take his place.

INTERNET LINK

At www.usborne-quicklinks.com you'll find a link to a site where you can follow a Web quest, which investigates Tutankhamun's death and asks, "Was it Murder?"

A painting of Akhenaten's daughters, painted in the Amarna style (see page 27).

A DEADLY PLAGUE?

After Tutankhamun's death, a strange thing happened. His young widow Ankhesenpaamun wrote to the king of the Hittites, Egypt's rivals, begging him to send her a husband. The Hittite king obliged, but his son never arrived – he was assassinated on the way.

This story is unusual, as royal Egyptian women didn't usually marry foreigners. However, the queen stated in her letter that she didn't want to marry a 'servant'. This could refer to the old man Ay, who was of lower rank. Another explanation for the shortage of suitable husbands may have been a terrible plague that killed many Egyptians and Hittites, and possibly members of the royal households. This might solve another mystery, too: all Akhenaten's other daughters disappeared without trace.

One of Tutankhamun's thrones shows Ankhesenpaamun rubbing the king with ointment.

MURDER?

Ay reigned for only four years. When he died, a powerful army general named Horemheb wasted no time in grasping the throne. He was a ruthless man who tried to wipe Akhenaten, Tutankhamun and Ay from memory – their names and images were hacked from paintings and sculptures. The finger of guilt also points to Horemheb as the murderer of the Hittite prince.

In Tutankhamun's tomb, Ay is shown performing the ceremony of the Opening of the Mouth (see page 61). This was usually carried out by the dead king's son and heir.

THE REIGN OF HOREMHEB

Despite his shadowy background, Horemheb ruled steadily for about 28 years. He reformed the army, made sure all Egypt's boundaries were made secure, and restored order to local and central government. He also claimed to have carried out a lot of building work – but in fact simply took the credit for Tutankhamun's.

Horemheb

RAMESSES II

The 18th Dynasty came to an end with the reign of Horemheb, who appointed a man named Ramesses to follow him as pharaoh and begin the 19th dynasty. This dynasty's third king, Ramesses II, had an extraordinary reign. He lived longer than almost any other pharaoh. He was also a great self-publicist, who created as big a name for himself as possible.

Ramesses I, shown here being greeted by gods in the afterlife, was the first of many Ramesses.

RAMESSES I AND SETI I

Ramesses I was an army officer before he became king. He was already old, and reigned for only two years before his son Seti I took over. Seti decided to rebuild the Egyptian empire, which had been lost during the reign of Akhenaten. He led several campaigns to conquer Palestine, reaching right up into Syria and conflicting with the Hittites to the north. But each time he won and returned home, his enemies crept back into the territory he had gained.

A LEGENDARY REIGN

Seti I's son, Ramesses II, had one of the longest reigns in history. He reigned for over 67 years and was probably in his late eighties when he died. He had many wives and children in the course of his long reign. His chief queen, Nefertari, was evidently very well loved and respected. Ramesses had a temple built especially for her at Abu Simbel, and she also had her own beautiful tomb in the Valley of the Queens (see page 69).

A granite statue of Ramesses II holding the royal crook

PROPAGANDA

Ramesses II was a master of the art of propaganda. For one thing, he claimed that the god Amun was his real father. He also commissioned colossal building projects, such as the Ramesseum (his mortuary temple), the hypostyle hall at Karnak, and the majestic temples of Abu Simbel. However, many other buildings were simply adapted to make it look as though he had built them himself.

 INTERNET LINK

At **www.usborne-quicklinks.com** you'll find a link to the **Ancient Egypt Magazine Web site**, where you can read an exciting imaginary account of the Battle of Kadesh.

THE HITTITES

Ramesses II continued his father's campaign to recapture the Egyptian empire in Palestine and Syria. This soon led to renewed hostilities with the Hittites. In the fifth year of his reign, Ramesses took on the Hittite army along the frontier of Egyptian territory at a place called Kadesh in Syria. He claimed this battle to be a great victory, even though the Egyptian army only narrowly escaped a heavy defeat. He had the battle depicted on the walls of many temples, including Abu Simbel and the hypostyle hall at Karnak.

The walls of the temple at Abu Simbel show Ramesses slaying his enemies in victorious battles.

TRAPPED AT KADESH

At the Battle of Kadesh, the Hittites tricked Ramesses into believing that they had retreated. They trapped one division of the Egyptian army – the Amun division, which had Ramesses at its head – but he showed great personal heroism in rallying his troops while waiting for reinforcements to arrive. He managed to hold out, and eventually both armies withdrew in stalemate.

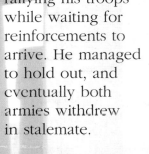

Amun division and Egyptian camp

Kadesh

Hittite attack

Re division

River Orontes

Map of the battlefield

In the Battle of Kadesh, Ramesses (wearing the blue khephresh war helmet) startled the Hittites by charging at them fearlessly.

A TREATY AND A WIFE

After further disputes, Ramesses came to an agreement with the Hittite king and they signed a treaty. To seal this new friendship, Ramesses married a Hittite princess. This peace lasted throughout the rest of his reign and beyond, until the Hittite kingdom collapsed in c.1196BC.

A NEW CAPITAL

Because of Egypt's interest in Palestine and Syria, Ramesses decided he needed a capital nearer to them. The new capital, Per Ramesses, was built on the site of the Hyksos capital, Avaris. Poets wrote about the beauty of this city, which remained the capital until the end of the New Kingdom.

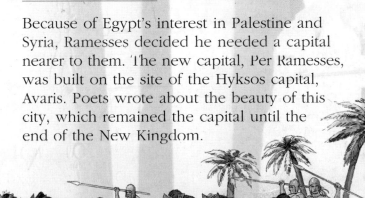

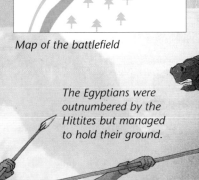

The Egyptians were outnumbered by the Hittites but managed to hold their ground.

THE NEW KINGDOM ENDS

Things would never be the same again after Ramesses II died. The 19th dynasty collapsed within only a few decades. Other New Kingdom kings tried to recreate the glory of his reign, often by taking his name, which meant the 20th dynasty was dominated by kings called Ramesses. But none was able to match him. The New Kingdom came to an end and the Third Intermediate Period began.

FOREIGN THREATS

Ramesses' successor Merenptah had to face new threats to Egypt's security The first came from the west, what is now Libya. Many people starting arriving, hoping to settle in the Delta – probably because of famine. Merenptah had to drive them back.

The second threat was more dangerous. Groups from around the Mediterranean formed what the Egyptians called the 'Sea Peoples' and tried to invade Egypt. Merenptah defeated them, killing 6,000, but more were to return 20 years later.

RAMESSES III

The 20th dynasty's second king, Ramesses III, tried to be as great as his namesake, Ramesses II, but he had to deal with many problems. Libyans tried to invade again, and many settled in the Delta. The Sea Peoples attempted another massive invasion, too, and Ramesses battled with them at sea and on land. He won, but Egypt was weakened by the battles and soon lost much of its empire.

A Peleset warrior, one of the Sea Peoples

THE FIRST STRIKE

Ramesses III carried out a few building projects, including his mortuary temple at Medinet Habu. But his administration was not very efficient and he didn't pay his workers. So they went on strike – the first recorded strike in history.

CONSPIRACY

Even Ramesses' family caused him problems. One of his wives led a conspiracy to kill him and replace him with her son. The plan didn't work and there was a huge trial. Many people were found guilty and at least 17 were executed. Others were allowed to kill themselves, or had their ears and noses chopped off. In the end, Ramesses III was succeeded by a different son. There were another seven Ramesses in the 20th dynasty, but none was very impressive.

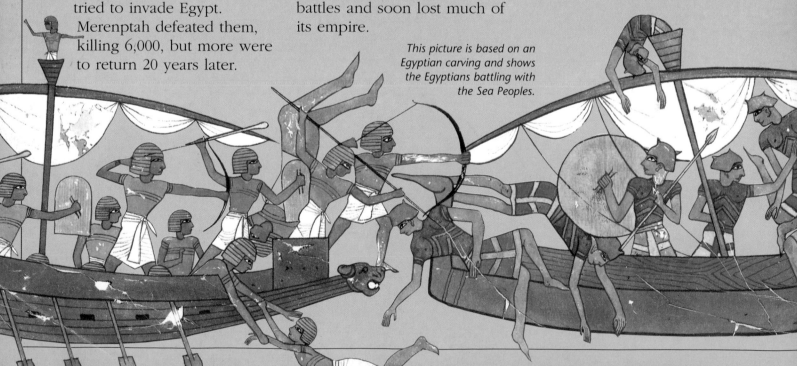

This picture is based on an Egyptian carving and shows the Egyptians battling with the Sea Peoples.

TOMB RAIDERS

During the reign of Ramesses IX, a scandal broke that ran for 20 years. Nobles' tombs were being robbed, and a few royal tombs, too. The great scandal was that some of the robbers actually worked in the local temples. Even the mayor of Thebes was suspected, and there was a big trial.

Tomb raiders ransacked the tombs as quickly as they could.

But no one important was found guilty. The convicted robbers were sentenced to a gruesome death – by impalement (being stuck on a spike).

Despite the trial, the problem of tomb robberies continued, especially of the royal tombs. So, in the 21st dynasty, priests decided to move the most important mummies to keep them safe. Two of these were Ramesses II and Seti I, who were hidden in a 'cache' at Deir el Bahri. Others were hidden in the tomb of Amenhotep II in the Valley of the Kings.

The mummies shown here are Seti I, Ramesses IV and Ramesses II, all found in the 'cache' of mummies at Deir el Bahri.

OFFICIALS' POWER

None of the last kings of the 20th dynasty was very strong, and the government structure began to collapse. Nubia broke away, and administration became very disorganized. Because the kings themselves were so weak, officials such as army generals, viziers and priests began to wield more power. By the end of the 20th dynasty, a general called Heri-Hor was more or less ruling Egypt. He also took the title of high priest at Thebes.

⬥ INTERNET LINK

At **www.usborne-quicklinks.com** you'll find a link to a Web site where you can read a detailed feature article all about the robberies of the royal tombs of ancient Egypt.

A MELTING POT

Egypt's days of glory were now long past. As the New Kingdom stumbled to an end, the Third Intermediate Period ushered in a time of confusion and division, followed by wave after wave of foreign rulers.

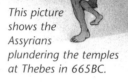

This picture shows the Assyrians plundering the temples at Thebes in 665BC.

TANIS AND THEBES

Ramesses XI died in c.1069BC, leaving two powerful men – Smendes in the capital (Per Ramesses), and Pinudjem, the high priest, at Thebes. They were probably both sons of Heri-Hor.

NILE DELTA

Tanis

WESTERN DESERT

This map shows the location of Tanis in relation to Thebes.

Nile

Thebes

Smendes made himself king and moved the capital to Tanis, founding the 21st dynasty. Tanis was built along similar lines to Thebes, with temples to Amun and Mut. Pinudjem recognized Smendes as king for a while, then proclaimed himself king as well. After this, Egyptian rule remained divided between Tanis and Thebes for over 100 years.

The kings of Tanis were buried there. Beautiful treasures have been found at the site, such as this silver coffin belonging to Psusennes I, a 21st dynasty king.

THE LIBYANS

As the dynasty of kings ruling at Tanis began to crumble, powerful Libyan settlers living in the Delta grasped the chance to become rulers. These Libyan pharaohs formed the 22nd dynasty.

The first Libyan ruler, Shoshenq I, married his son to the heiress of Tanis and was Commander-in-Chief of the army before taking the title of pharaoh in c.945BC. He appointed one of his sons as high priest at Thebes. By doing this, he more or less united Egypt again.

The gold mask on the right is made of a single sheet of gold. It was found at Tanis and belonged to Shoshenq II, one of the 22nd dynasty Libyan kings.

THE EMPIRE REGAINED?

The Libyan rulers were keen to establish the Egyptian empire to the east once more, and Shoshenq I carried out some successful raids in Palestine. He looted the city of Jerusalem in c.925BC, carrying off much of the treasure in its main temple. But Egyptian power was never really restored permanently in the region.

Assyrian soldiers were very violent and bloodthirsty and killed many Egyptians.

The Assyrians carried off all the gold in the temples.

What they couldn't take with them, the Assyrians tried to burn instead.

RULERS FROM NUBIA

The Libyan period ended in confusion, with many princes ruling at once. Meanwhile the Nubians, who had freed themselves of Egyptian rule in the reign of Ramesses XI, pushed north in c.728BC, led by a man named Piankhi.

The Nubians had adopted many Egyptian customs, and were more fervent Amun-worshippers than the Egyptians themselves. So Piankhi set himself up at Thebes, starting the 25th dynasty. He fought the princes in the Delta until they all recognized him as king of Egypt.

This sphinx has the face of Taharqa, a 25th dynasty Nubian king.

THE RISE OF ASSYRIA

During the Nubian period, the balance of power in the Near East was changing yet again. The Assyrians had become the major power, and by c.750BC they controlled a large part of Mesopotamia and Palestine. The Nubian kings joined forces with kings in Palestine to try to push them back – but only drew the Assyrians' attention to Egypt instead. The Assyrians invaded the Delta twice, but the Nubian kings continued to rebel. Eventually the Assyrians decided to teach Egypt a lesson.

THE SACK OF THEBES

With the help of princes from the Delta, the Assyrians marched as far as Thebes in 665 BC. They plundered the temples and set them alight. The Nubian king of the time, Tanutamen, was forced to flee back to Nubia, bringing Nubian rule in Egypt to an end.

 INTERNET LINK

At **www.usborne-quicklinks.com** there's a link to the **British Museum Mesopotamia Web site**, where you can find out more about the ancient Assyrians and their armies.

THE LAST KINGS

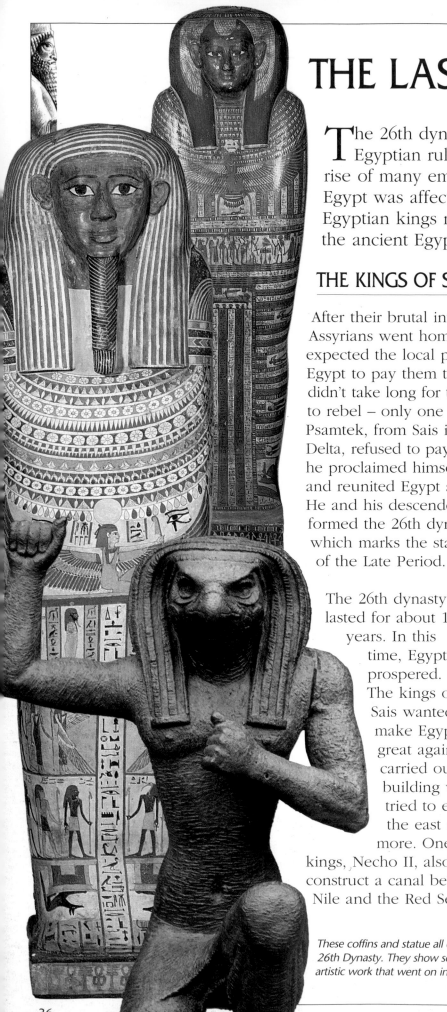

The 26th dynasty was the last great dynasty of native Egyptian rulers. The final six centuries BC saw the rise of many empires in the Near East and Europe, and Egypt was affected by all of them. In the 4th century BC, Egyptian kings ruled again, but only briefly. After this, the ancient Egyptian civilization was taken over for good.

THE KINGS OF SAIS

After their brutal invasion, the Assyrians went home, but still expected the local princes of Egypt to pay them tribute. It didn't take long for the princes to rebel – only one year later, Psamtek, from Sais in the Delta, refused to pay. In 664BC he proclaimed himself king and reunited Egypt again. He and his descendents formed the 26th dynasty, which marks the start of the Late Period.

The 26th dynasty lasted for about 150 years. In this time, Egypt prospered. The kings of Sais wanted to make Egypt great again, so they carried out a lot of building work and tried to expand to the east once more. One of these kings, Necho II, also started to construct a canal between the Nile and the Red Sea.

These coffins and statue all date from the 26th Dynasty. They show some of the fine artistic work that went on in this period.

PERSIAN TYRANNY

The next great empire to conquer Egypt was that of the Persians. By 525BC, they had defeated the last king of Sais, Psamtek III. They then took control of Egypt for the next 120 years or so, ruling through a *satrap* or local governer. The Persians were very unpopular rulers, even though they ruled from a distance – the only one to visit Egypt personally was Cambyses II. However, the emperor Darius, who followed Cambyses, did make an effort to be fair and to respect Egyptian customs.

The Persian emperor Darius

GREEK SETTLERS

During the Late Period, more and more Greeks came to live in Egypt, first as merchants but later as mercenaries. They were fascinated by Egyptian culture and adopted many Egyptian practices. They also provided Egypt with soldiers. In the Persian Period, Egypt formed a number of alliances with Greece.

Alexander the Great, shown on an ancient Roman mosaic

 INTERNET LINK

At **www.usborne-quicklinks.com** you'll find a link to the **University of South Florida Alexandria Web site,** where you can find out all about the city founded by Alexander the Great.

LAST EGYPTIAN KINGS

The Egyptians constantly rebelled against the Persians and in about 404BC, they managed to get rid of their hated rulers for a while.

This brief, final period of Egyptian independence lasted only about 60 years, but these years were certainly eventful. There were many wars, as the Greeks and Egyptians constantly tried to ward off the Persian threat. Eventually, the Persians invaded again under Ataxerxes II, and the last Egyptian king, Nectanebo II, was forced to flee.

King Nectanebo II making an offering. He had a reputation as a great magician.

ALEXANDER THE GREAT

In 334BC, another empire was rising – that of Alexander the Great, based in Macedonia (northern Greece). He swept into Egypt and ousted the Persians in 332BC. The Egyptians welcomed him as a hero, and an oracle declared him a son of Amun. Alexander founded a new capital, named Alexandria, on the Mediterranean coast. Then, in 323BC, aged only 32, he died. His empire was divided between three generals. One called Ptolemy (say 'Tollomy') took control of Egypt.

PTOLEMY TAKES OVER

Ptolemy and his descendents ruled Egypt for nearly 300 years. All these kings were called Ptolemy, and their queens were called Cleopatra, Arsinoe or Berenice.

The Ptolemies spoke Greek, and made Greek the official language. They saw Greek culture as superior, but at least they lived in Egypt and tried to please their Egyptian subjects. They respected the old traditions and carried out a lot of building work in the Egyptian style.

This is part of the temple of Isis at Philae. This temple was rebuilt in the Ptolemaic period.

THE LAST QUEEN

Although Cleopatra was one of the most important queens of Egypt, she wasn't even Egyptian. She was a Ptolemy, so her origins were Greek. But she was the last ruler of Egypt before it lost independence. She was born there, and her story shows that she saw Egypt as home.

A coin showing Mark Antony's head

Shows the size of the Roman Empire in 31BC, the year of the battle of Actium.

FRANCE

ITALY
Rome

GREECE
Actium

SPAIN

Cleopatra and Antony fled from Actium to Egypt.

Alexandria

EGYPT

THE ROMANS

By about 100BC, a new force was gaining power all around the Mediterranean – the Romans. As the Romans grew in strength, Alexander's Macedonian empire slowly crumbled under the pressure. It wasn't long before the Ptolemies were forced to acknowledge the power of Rome. For the time being, the Roman senators just dabbled in Egyptian politics, and allowed the Ptolemies to remain rulers. But this was about to change, too.

CLEOPATRA VII

Cleopatra VII became queen in 51BC, as the wife of her young brother, Ptolemy XIII. She hadn't wanted to marry him and she soon quarrelled with his advisers. The situation grew worse, until war broke out. The Roman general Julius Caesar came to Alexandria to sort things out. Cleopatra won Caesar over to her side – in fact, he became her lover.

Ptolemy was killed, and Cleopatra became sole ruler of Egypt. But then Caesar was murdered, so Cleopatra joined forces with one of his friends, Mark Antony, and became his lover, too. Octavian, Caesar's heir, didn't want any rivals to the east, and war broke out. Cleopatra and Mark Antony were defeated by his army at the Battle of Actium in 31BC.

To avoid more humiliation, both Mark Antony and Cleopatra killed themselves. He used a sword but, so the story goes, Cleopatra used an asp (a poisonous snake). After this, Egypt became part of the Roman Empire.

*Elizabeth Taylor as Cleopatra in the film **Cleopatra**. Behind her is an artist's impression of the Battle of Actium, in which Antony and Cleopatra were defeated by Octavian.*

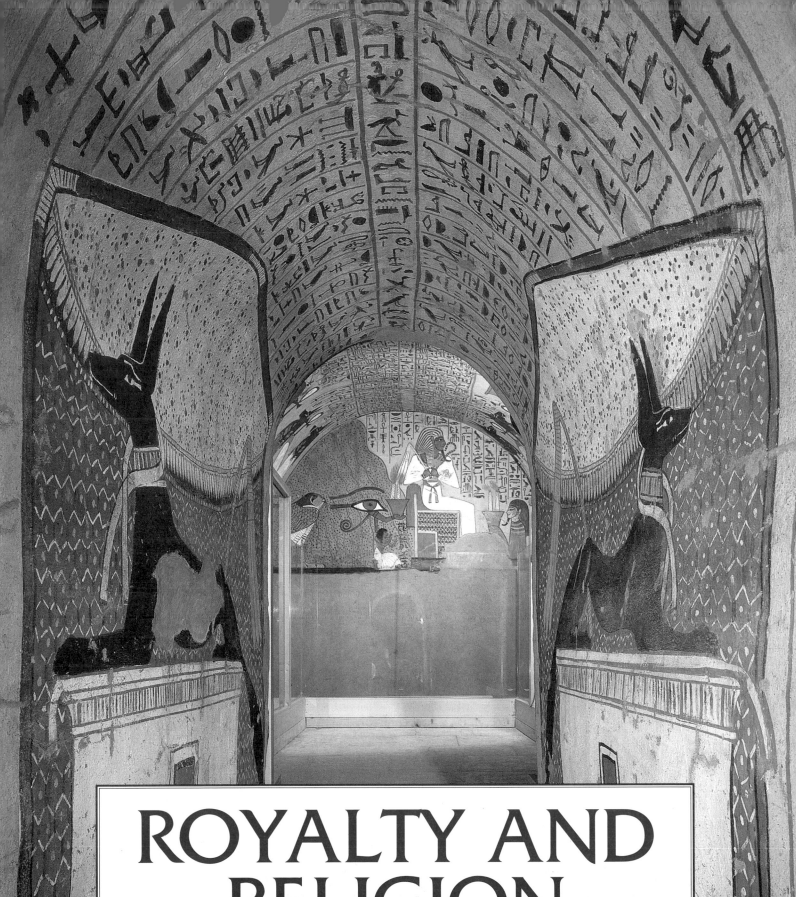

ROYALTY AND RELIGION

THE ROLE OF KING

The king was far more than just a ruler. He represented the gods, and had absolute power. People even believed he could make it rain. But he still had to abide by the principle of *ma'at*, or justice and mercy.

DIVINE ORIGINS

Originally, so it was said, Egypt was ruled by the gods, who lived on Earth like people. Horus, the falcon god, was king, and Osiris ruled the Next World. When the gods no longer ruled on earth, Horus sent his spirit to enter the king instead. When he died, the king became one with Osiris, and the role of Horus passed to the next king.

THE KING'S NAME

The king was considered so important that people didn't refer to him directly. They spoke of the 'Palace' or 'per-aa' instead. This is the origin of the title 'pharaoh'. Kings had two different names: their 'Son of Re' name, received at birth, and their *nsw-bity* name, received when they were crowned. *Nsw-bity* means 'King of Upper and Lower Egypt'. We usually refer to kings by their Son of Re name.

Tutankhamun's head and shoulders from his solid gold coffin. He is holding a crook and flail, and has a cobra and vulture at his forehead.

CROWNING GLORY

The king is often shown wearing either the Red Crown of Lower Egypt or the White Crown of Upper Egypt, or a double crown.

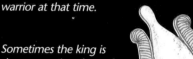

By the New Kingdom, a new bright blue crown had appeared, called the khephresh. It was more of a battle helmet than a crown, and reflects the importance of the king's role as warrior at that time.

Khephresh

Sometimes the king is shown wearing the atef crown – a tall crown adorned with ostrich feathers, which had more religious significance.

Atef

Kings also wore a menes, or long striped head-dress. Like other crowns, this had a vulture's head and a cobra's head attached to it, to represent Nekhmet and Wadjet, the king's protectors.

Menes

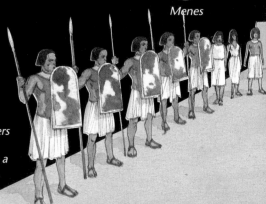

ROYAL REGALIA

In paintings and carvings, kings are often shown holding some kind of royal regalia (symbolic item). The most important were the crook and flail. The crook was used by shepherds, so symbolized the king's protection of his people. The flail was used to whip people, so symbolized the king's punishment of his enemies.

There was also a selection of other symbolic items: in scenes of war, the king usually carries a mace (a stick with a stone ball on the end) to smite his enemies. In the afterlife, he holds the *ankh*, a kind of cross that meant 'life', which many of the gods are shown holding, too.

A war mace and an ankh, the symbol of life.

SYMBOLIC POWER

Egyptian art sometimes demonstrates the king's power by showing him as a powerful animal, such as a lion or sphinx. This was a reminder that he was a god, who could appear in many forms.

The king was also represented as a strong bull, which gave rise to the 'Festival of the Tail' – the Heb Sed. Part of the king's costume was actually a bull's tail, which you can see in some pictures.

During the Sed festival, the king had to perform physical activities, such as a ceremonial run, to renew his strength and show that he was still fit. Sed festivals were supposed to happen when a king had reigned for thirty years. But kings often held them more often, especially if their strength was failing or after some kind of disaster.

The Heb Sed festival taking place in the big courtyard in front of the Step Pyramid at Saqqara. The king runs around to prove he is still fit.

THE ROLE OF QUEENS

The king was almost always a man. He had one chief queen and many minor ones. The chief queen was often the king's sister or half-sister. In early statues and carvings, queens are often shown very small, because they were much less important than the king. But in the New Kingdom they became more important, and were seen as the divine incarnation of the goddess Hathor, Horus's wife.

King Hatshepsut was a woman, here shown as a sphinx to demonstrate her power.

Like all ceremonies in Egypt, the Heb Sed had religious significance and was attended by priests.

White crown of Lower Egypt

GOVERNMENT AND POWER

Even though the king had absolute power, in practice he was surrounded by ministers who did a lot of the work for him. The government of Ancient Egypt was very well organized, with lots of departments and officials. There were strict ways of doing things and everything was written down.

HOW GOVERNMENT WORKED

Ancient Egyptian government was 'centralized', which meant that the king made all the important decisions. When there was a king who wasn't very good at this, the whole government ran into problems.

The king's decisions were carried out by his ministers. Becoming a minister wasn't easy, as most top jobs stayed within families. But if your parents paid for an education and you were talented enough, it was possible to work your way up.

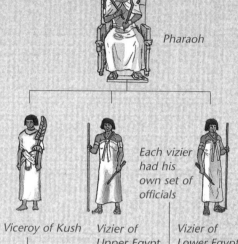

Pharaoh

Each vizier had his own set of officials

Viceroy of Kush *Vizier of Upper Egypt* *Vizier of Lower Egypt*

Viceroy staff *Treasury* *Granaries* *Royal Works* *Army* *Priesthood*

This diagram shows how the government was structured, with the viziers below the king and everyone else below them.

GOVERNMENT DEPARTMENTS

After the king, the two viziers (for Upper and Lower Egypt) were the most important officials, along with the Viceroy of Kush, who governed Nubia. The viziers were in charge of all government departments and the justice system. They had to collect taxes, supervise irrigation and building projects, receive visitors and much, much more. Below the viziers were the army, the priesthood and overseers of several other departments. The biggest were the Treasury, Granaries and Royal Works (building projects).

In this wall painting, government officials measure how much a peasant should pay the king in tax.

TAXES AND MONEY

Until the Persian Period, Egypt didn't have coins or money as we know it. People paid for things – including their taxes – 'in kind', which means with goods or work. They had to give part of whatever they grew or made to the government, and some of their time, too.

The Egyptian work tax is now described as a 'corvée'. Corvées were very well organized, and were used for many tasks, from digging irrigation channels to carrying out building projects. In fact, if it wasn't for the corvées, the pyramids would never have been built.

PRIESTS AND GENERALS

Two other major aspects of Egyptian life provided some top jobs. These were the army (mainly from the New Kingdom onwards) and the temples.

This striking sycamore statue, found on the West Bank at Thebes, is of a priest named Ka-aper.

The king depended on the army to maintain Egypt's strength, so army generals had a lot of power and influence. They sometimes even became king themselves. Horemheb and Ramesses I are two examples.

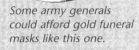

Some army generals could afford gold funeral masks like this one.

The temples were important for administration as well as worship, and they collected taxes on behalf of the king. As a result, High Priests had a lot of influence.

 INTERNET LINK

*At **www.usborne-quicklinks.com** you'll find a link to the **Cleveland Museum of Art Web site**, which gives fiddly but fun instructions for making your own pharaoh's mask.*

WAS IT FAIR?

Overall, ordinary people were treated well in this system, and they could go to court to settle disputes. People accused of crimes received a fair trial, though they might be beaten to test whether they were telling the truth. There were local and district courts, but if these courts were unable to resolve a dispute, the matter could go before the vizier or even the king himself. Watching trials was a popular public pastime.

Convicted criminals faced a range of punishments. If a crime was serious, they could be executed or mutilated (have their nose, ears or hands cut off). Less serious crimes were punished with floggings, fines, or sometimes exile to a remote place.

In a local court, a panel of judges would decide whether or not the accused was guilty of the crime.

Scribes made records of all that happened.

The accused man had to listen to the charges, but he was allowed to defend himself.

This man reads the charges against the accused.

FIGHTING FORCES

Egypt's army varied enormously in the course of its history. There were times when there wasn't a national army at all, and times when there were several small ones. During the New Kingdom, though, Egypt's army was truly impressive, and struck terror into many other peoples of the Near East.

Golden flies, such as these, were used as symbols of military glory. They were given to reward bravery in battle.

EARLY ARMIES

In the Old Kingdom, Egypt only had a small professional army. In the provinces, local rulers had bands of men that the king could called on if he needed to. It's likely that the first full national army was established by Middle Kingdom kings in the 12th dynasty. They wanted to make sure that Egypt didn't splinter apart in a hurry. However, at this stage the army was probably still quite small.

This group of model Nubian soldiers was found in a Middle Kingdom tomb.

MEN FROM NUBIA

From as early as the 6th dynasty, men from Nubia moved north into Egypt to join the army. Men who are paid to fight on behalf of a foreign country like this are called mercenaries. In the New Kingdom, one Nubian tribe named the Medjay concentrated more on keeping law and order than on fighting other countries. Because of this, the word 'Medjay' eventually came to mean police force.

The soldiers are carrying bows and arrows, as Nubians were famous for their skill as archers.

ARMY STRUCTURE

In the New Kingdom, Egypt went to war regularly. New weapons and chariots were introduced, and the army became a key part of the Egyptian hierarchy. The king was Commander-in-Chief, but there was a whole range of posts beneath him, from royal battle adviser to the humble job of distributing supplies to the soldiers. There was also a navy, for transporting troops and suppressing attacks along the Mediterranean coast.

The New Kingdom army was divided into units, each named after an Egyptian god (for example, Amun, Re, or Set). Every unit had 4,000 foot soldiers and 500 chariots, each with two men – one to drive, the other to fight.

In battle, experienced soldiers fought at the front, with newer recruits behind them. The quick-moving chariots went wherever they were needed. The role of trumpeters and standard-bearers (men carrying flags that soldiers could see) became important for keeping everyone together and passing on orders.

This wall painting shows soldiers in their barracks. Some are being given their weapons, while others are having their hair cut short.

HARDSHIP AND REWARD

Army life was tough. Soldiers were sent on long marches and had to take part in regular wrestling matches. Battles were gruesome, bloody affairs that could leave a soldier horribly maimed or disfigured – if he even survived. But there were definite advantages to being in the army. Soldiers were rewarded for bravery with precious objects such as gold or silver weapons, jewels, or medals in the shape of flies. They also received a share of plunder whenever they defeated an enemy.

The mummy of Seqenenre Tao, a Theban prince who fought against the Hyksos, shows terrible head wounds – probably received in battle.

Part of an Egyptian army division. The charioteers are shown at the front with neat lines of foot soldiers behind them.

TRADE AND DIPLOMACY

The relationship between Egypt and nearby lands was a very complex one. As well as maintaining its power in the region, Egypt needed to guard the trade routes that provided it with vital goods. As a result, Egyptian kings kept tight control of trade coming in and out of the country, and their messengers and ambassadors often dealt with trade agreements as well as diplomatic matters.

GOODS IN AND OUT

Egypt had plenty of resources to trade. It exported grain, wine, linen, papyrus, and manufactured goods. In particular, it was famous for its gold. One of the Amarna letters (see right) shows that other nations thought Egypt was almost dripping with it – 'Send me gold, gold and more gold, for in my Brother's land gold is as the dust,' it says. In fact, the gold came mainly from Nubia.

In return, Egypt imported many goods from the Near East, Greece and Cyprus – oil and resin, silver, copper, slaves and horses; while from Punt it received myrrh trees and other exotic African goods. From the leafy mountains of Lebanon came something that in Egypt was in very short supply – wood.

GREECE

Egypt imported wine, oil and silver from Greece and its surrounding islands.

This map shows the main trade routes going in and out of Egypt.

Copper was beaten into shapes like this.

LEBANON

Cyprus supplied opium and copper.

CYPRUS

MEDITERRANEAN SEA

Salt and dates came from the desert oases.

Cedar wood was shipped to Egypt from Lebanon.

SINAI

Nearby Sinai was a good source of copper and turquoise, which were imported by donkey.

Grain and papyrus were two of Egypt's major exports.

Egypt relied heavily on Nubia for its rich supplies of gold, which it then exported.

EGYPT

Ivory came from the African interior.

NUBIA

THE TALE OF WEN-AMUN

The Tale of Wen-Amun was written at the end of the New Kingdom (c.1070BC). It tells the story of an Egyptian ambassador, and shows the links between the worlds of trade and diplomacy.

Wen-Amun was sent on a mission to Byblos in Lebanon to collect some cedar wood, but he was robbed on the way.

Then, when he eventually arrived, he was treated very badly by the authorities in Byblos. Eventually they agreed to give him the wood he needed, but only at a very high price. The story shows how Egypt's power was beginning to wane at the end of the New Kingdom. Other nations weren't afraid of upsetting the Egyptians any more.

FOREIGN TRIBUTE

In the New Kingdom, Egypt's wealth was increased by foreign tribute that conquered nations had to pay. The conquered peoples resented this, and often rebelled. So Egypt adopted 'diplomatic' ploys to encourage payment. One was to take foreign princes' children and bring them to Egypt. They were well treated and educated, so that when they went home they promoted a positive attitude towards their Egyptian rulers.

Nubia, though, was different. It was a conquered territory for much of Egyptian history, and special to Egypt because of its gold. The Nubians did rebel at first, but gradually accepted the benefits of being linked to Egypt and adopted Egyptian customs as their own.

Everyone was obliged to show great respect in the presence of the Egyptian king.

The Egyptians expected to be given the very best goods as tribute.

African traders arriving with ivory, animal skins, baboons and other goods

In this carving, a Libyan captive is brought to Egypt, his hands tied behind his back.

INTERNET LINK

At **www.usborne-quicklinks.com** *you'll find a link to a Web site where you can read a detailed account of* The Tale of Wen-Amun, *translated from the original hieroglyphs.*

THE AMARNA LETTERS

The Amarna letters are about 350 baked clay tablets, found in the ruins of Akhetaten (see page 26). They are mainly letters written to the king of Egypt from the kings and princes of Assyria, Babylonia, Mitanni, Cyprus, Palestine, Syria and Hatti (the Hittites).

The tablets are written in cuneiform script, (wedge-like shapes), and in Akkadian, the diplomatic language of the day. The more powerful kings called the Egyptian king 'Brother', but their letters could

The clay Amarna letters were small enough for a messenger to carry around his neck.

get very frosty – in one, the king of Mitanni is furious with the king of Egypt for detaining a Mitanni messenger for six years. Lesser kings addressed the Egyptian king with more respect, calling him 'My God', or 'The Great King'. They begged for help, or tried to turn Egypt against their rivals.

THE EGYPTIAN RELIGION

Egyptian religion was a big tangle of beliefs rather than one simple idea. Very early in Egyptian history, in the Predynastic Period, dozens of different gods appeared. Some were only worshipped in people's homes, some in particular areas, while others were worshipped throughout Egypt. There were many myths, too, which varied enormously – even the best-known had different versions.

In this painting, the sun god Re makes his mythical daily journey across the sky in his boat.

WHAT THE GODS WERE LIKE

Most Egyptian gods were gods of a specific object or activity, such as embalming (Anubis), the moon (Khonsu) or water (Sobek). Some, though, represented more abstract ideas such as justice and harmony (Ma'at) or wisdom (Thoth). Many were associated with a particular animal, bird or plant, and were often represented in more than one way. For example, Hathor is sometimes shown as a cow, a woman, or a woman with the head or ears of a cow.

A statue of Anubis, the god of embalming

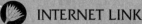 **INTERNET LINK**

Go to **www.usborne-quicklinks.com** for a link to the **British Museum's Ancient Egypt Web site**, where you can find out more about all the different gods and goddesses.

THE CREATION MYTH

The best-known Egyptian creation story developed in the city of Heliopolis. Originally, so the story went, there was nothing but chaos. Out of this, the sun-god Re (or Ra) created himself, then created everything else. First of all he created Shu (air) and Tefnut (moisture). Shu and Tefnut had two children, Geb (the earth) and Nut (the sky).

Osiris

Isis

Geb and Nut had four children: Osiris, Isis, Set and Nephthys. You can read a version of their story opposite. Osiris and Isis were the parents of the falcon god Horus, and Nephthys also had a child by Osiris – Anubis, the jackal-headed god of embalming. Horus's wife was Hathor, the goddess of love, happiness and childbirth.

Nephthys

Every day, Re sailed across the sky in his barque, or boat. Each night, he sailed through the underworld where he had to defeat the monstrous god of darkness, Apep, in order to rise again in the morning.

Hathor

OSIRIS AND ISIS

Osiris took the place of his father Geb on the throne, and ruled fairly and justly. But his brother Set was jealous, and decided to kill him. He made a coffin that only Osiris would fit into, tricked him into getting inside, then quickly shut the lid and threw the coffin into the Nile. It floated away to the sea, and Set was sure he had defeated his brother.

But Isis, the sister-wife of Osiris, wouldn't rest until she found his body. She found the coffin and took it back to Egypt. Set was furious. He hunted down the body, cut it into fourteen pieces, then

In the final battle between Horus and Set, Horus won, but not before losing an eye.

buried each piece in a different place along the Nile. Even so, Isis didn't give up. With the help of her sister Nephthys, she found all but one of the pieces, and Anubis helped her to put Osiris back together again. He came to life briefly, and became the father of Horus. Then Re made him king of the Underworld.

Isis protected Horus from Set by hiding him in the reeds on the Nile until he was old enough to avenge his father's death. After a long battle, Horus defeated Set and became king of Egypt. So Egyptians believed that the spirit of Horus entered every king, and that when the king died, his spirit went to the Next World and was joined to the spirit of Osiris instead.

An udjat *eye, or Eye of Horus*

THE EYE OF HORUS

One of the Egyptians' best-loved amulets was the *udjat* eye, or 'Eye of Horus'. In his battle with Set, Horus lost an eye, and the god Thoth healed it. So this eye became a symbol for healing, and was believed to bring good health and fitness. It was also a symbol of sacrifice, because Horus had lost it when he was battling against evil.

MORE ABOUT MYTHS

Over the years, the Egyptian religion kept on changing and evolving. Gods would rise to greater importance and then fade into the background, while myths evolved or merged together. Some changes were more significant than others, though, and were often a reflection of the shifts in power that were taking place. For example, the rise of Thebes had a big impact on religion across the country.

The goddess Ma'at is often shown with outstretched wings, to represent balance and harmony.

THE HERMOPOLIS MYTH

The city of Hermopolis had its own creation myth, in which the world was originally ruled by Ma'at (goddess of justice, order and truth) and her husband Thoth, the ibis-headed god of scribes and wisdom. They had four sets of twins – Nun and Nanuet, Heh and Hehet, Kek and Keket, and Amun and Amunet.

These eight gods were the forces of creation. Of the eight, only Amun became a major god, but Ma'at and Thoth were important throughout Egypt. They had a special role in deciding people's fate in the afterlife, and they were both believed to stand by Re's boat each day as he voyaged across the sky.

Thoth

Amun

Mut

Khonsu

THE GODS OF THEBES

By the end of the Old Kingdom, Amun had been adopted as the god of Thebes. Until the New Kingdom, he was not particularly important elsewhere. Then, as Theban rulers came to power, the worship of Amun began to spread, until he was worshipped throughout Egypt.

Amun's wife was originally his twin, Amunet, but in Thebes she was replaced by Mut, the goddess of motherhood. Mut and Amun had a son called Khonsu, the moon god. Amun, Mut and Khonsu are known as the 'Theban Triad' (a triad is a group of three). As Amun-worship became more important and spread north from Thebes, Amun and Re were seen as the same god – Amun-Re, king of the gods.

50

THE RIVER OF BLOOD

In one myth, the god Re becomes angry with people for disobeying him and sends the lioness god Sekhmet to punish them. She begins to kill and eat people in a terrible slaughter. Re soon feels sorry for everyone, and regrets his judgement. He tries to stop Sekhmet, but she has developed a taste for blood and continues to destroy people. So, while she is asleep, Re pours beer into the river Nile, turning it red like blood.

When she awakes, Sekhmet thinks the river is flowing with blood, and so she drinks from it eagerly. But, because she is really drinking beer, she becomes drunk, and loses her desire to kill people. She is transformed into the goddess of love, Hathor, the wife of Horus (see page 48).

In the myth of Re and Sekhmet, Sekhmet is a terrifying lioness who kills all the people in her path.

(see page 48)

OTHER GODS

Sobek was the crocodile god, the god of water. He was worshipped in the Faiyum and at Kom Ombo.

Bast was the cat goddess, who represented the healing power of the Sun.

Khnum had a ram's head, and was a potter who made people on his potter's wheel.

Imhotep (see page 18) was one of the few non-royal people to be thought of as a god. He was worshipped by scribes, and as a god of medicine.

(see page 18)

TEMPLE LIFE

You can recognize priests in paintings because they had shaved heads. Here, a priest brings sacred water and incense to a noble in the afterlife.

Much of Egyptian life revolved around the big temples, although only the kings and priests could worship in the temple itself. Priests carried out many tasks, from teaching and administration to organizing building projects. Some worked in the temple full time, while others had jobs outside it.

TEMPLE LAYOUT

All temples had the same basic layout, because Egyptians believed the gods had designed the first temple when the world began.

Every temple was surrounded by an outer wall. The main gate (now known as a 'pylon') led into a courtyard. This was as far as ordinary people could go.

Beyond this point, the temples became increasingly dark, narrow and spooky. First there was the hypostyle hall, with columns built closely together to look like papyrus reeds. The only light came through little windows around the top.

Beyond this, the sanctuary or 'naos' was even darker. It held a statue of the god, usually stone, but often decorated with precious metal and jewels. Around the edge of the naos were annexes and storerooms.

Each temple also had a sacred lake, where the priests purified themselves.

BECOMING A PRIEST

In theory, the king was the only person who could approach the gods. But he couldn't be everywhere at once, which is why there were priests to stand in for him. Priests had to be educated, so becoming one wasn't easy.

Important priests worked in the temple full time, but most ordinary priests did another job for about eight months of the year. Some were kept busy with the administration and organization of temple life.

Priests took turns carrying out rituals. There were also priestesses, who gave responses in the services.

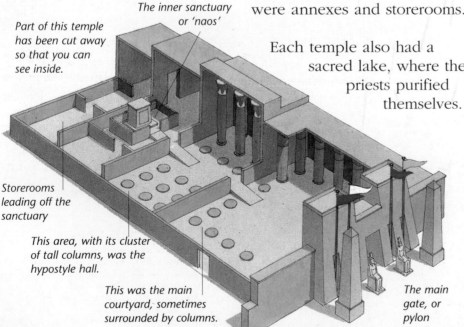

Part of this temple has been cut away so that you can see inside.

The inner sanctuary or 'naos'

Storerooms leading off the sanctuary

This area, with its cluster of tall columns, was the hypostyle hall.

This was the main courtyard, sometimes surrounded by columns.

The main gate, or pylon

THE DAILY RITUAL

The Egyptians believed that the gods sent part of their spirit into the statue in the temple, which the priests had to supply with plenty of food, drink and linen. Priests had to purify themselves by bathing in the sacred lake at least twice a day, and had to shave their whole body.

Every day, the priests woke the god with a hymn. Then they opened the sanctuary to bathe and dress the statue. Next came the offerings, of the best vegetables and meat, while incense was burned and singers and dancers provided entertainment. This ritual was repeated three times a day.

There were professional dancers and musicians in the temples.

During the day, the sanctuary doors were left open. You could peer from the main pylon right through to the sanctuary. At night, the priests closed the doors and backed off carefully. They swept away their footsteps as they went, in case a demon should make use of them overnight.

The priests and priestesses wore only the finest white linen.

Shafts of sunlight would have glinted dramatically from the ceiling-height windows, lighting up the huge pillars of the hypostyle hall.

 INTERNET LINK

Go to **www.usborne-quicklinks.com** *for a link to a Web site which tells you more about the different kinds of priests in Egyptian temples, and how they lived and worked.*

BUILDINGS FIT FOR GODS

The scale and grandeur of the ancient Egyptian temples was a reflection of the importance of both the gods and the king. Building them took thousands of men and incredible skill, using only very basic equipment.

MONUMENTAL STONE

Quarrying stone for building temples was a difficult, laborious job, so it was often prisoners of war or criminals who had to do it. Granite was the most difficult rock to quarry, because it was very hard. Limestone and sandstone were softer, so most temples were built from these. Granite was kept for details and specific objects, such as the tall spikes known as obelisks.

The Temple of Amun at Karnak is built mainly of easy-to-work limestone.

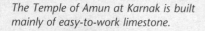

MUSCLE POWER

Hauling the huge blocks of stone to the temple sites needed hundreds of men. Rollers and ropes were used to drag the blocks to the river to be transported by boat. The Inundation helped, as it brought the river closer to the quarries. At the temple site, more men were needed to cut the stones to the right shape.

BUILDING BEGINS

The king himself attended a temple's foundation ceremony. He laid out the ground plan with posts and ropes, while the queen played the role of Sheshat, the goddess of writing, to record what he was doing.

After the ceremony, the first layer of stones was placed in position, and the area inside was filled with rubble. A ramp was made on the outside and the next layer of stones was hauled up. The inside was filled with more rubble and the ramp was raised for the third layer, and so on. Finally, a stone roof was placed over the top.

ARCHITECTURAL DETAILS

Once the temple was basically complete, the rubble and ramps were removed, level by level, so that craftsmen could start the decoration, from the top down. The stone columns were designed to look like palm tree trunks, or bundles of reeds. At the top and bottom, they were carved into the shape of lotus leaves and flowers, papyrus reeds or palm fronds.

Two examples of decoration

> **INTERNET LINK**
>
> *Go to www.usborne-quicklinks.com for a link to a Web site where you can zoom in on photographs of different temples around Egypt, and look at close-ups of their sculptures and reliefs.*

While the temple is still full of rubble, work begins on the decoration.

Craftsmen stood on the rubble to decorate the temple.

Taking away the rubble was a big job, and needed many men.

SCULPTURE

No temple was complete without big stone statues of the gods and king. First, the stone was shaped with hard stone pounders. Details of the face and clothing were sketched on the surface, then tapped out by a sculptor with copper and bronze chisels. The completed statues were covered with fine plaster and painted.

RELIEFS

Reliefs are the carvings that you see on the walls of temples. There were two main kinds – raised reliefs and sunken reliefs. For both, the carvers followed a design marked on the stone by a draftsman. Raised reliefs stood out from their backgrounds and were made by cutting away the surrounding stone. Sunken reliefs were made by cutting the figures and inscriptions deep into the stone. When the carvings were finished, they were painted in brilliant shades.

Raised relief

Sunken relief

THE RULES OF DESIGN

Egyptian design followed strict rules, based on a grid. A human figure always had the same proportions, and was divided into 18 parts or squares from head to toe (in the New Kingdom, this changed to 21 parts). Egyptians didn't copy what they saw, but drew what they knew was there. Shoulders and eyes were shown from the front, but the rest of the head, body and legs were shown from the side.

Craftsmen drawing out a scene using the grid

THE GREAT CULT TEMPLES

All the major Egyptian gods had temples along the Nile. These were called 'cult' temples, which just means they were dedicated to the worship of a particular god. Each site was that god's 'home', so new temples were simply built on the foundations of the old ones.

KARNAK AND LUXOR

The temple of Amun at Thebes, now called Karnak, is the biggest of all the temples still standing in Egypt. The complex as you see it today was started by Tuthmosis I, but many later kings added to it. Most of the additions were courtyards and pylons around the edges, so the oldest parts are in the middle.

Amun's consort, Mut, and his son Khonsu had their own temples at Karnak, too, and there was a big sacred lake. If you visit Karnak now, you can sit near the lake in the evening and watch a 'Sound and Light' show about the temple's history.

Luxor temple was another temple to Amun, not far from Karnak. Like Karnak, most of what you can see today was built during the New Kingdom. The two temples were originally connected by a magnificent avenue lined with sphinxes.

The temple of Luxor as it is today, with the Nile in the background.

EDFU AND DENDERA

As far back as the Old Kingdom, the main temple of Horus was at Edfu, and the temple of Hathor was at Dendera. The ones still standing today were built mainly by the Ptolemies.

These temples were linked by a major annual festival – the ceremonial marriage of the two gods. Hathor would travel on a barge all the way up the Nile to Edfu, and everyone would cheer her along the way from the banks.

OTHER TEMPLES

Today, we can only see a small number of the temples that once stood along the Nile. Temples in the Delta haven't lasted so well because the Nile Inundation tended to bury ruins under the rich river silt. There would have been a big temple to Re at Heliopolis, another to Ptah in Memphis, and many others.

Two that have survived, however, belonged to the cult of Isis at Philae, and to Sobek and Horus the Elder (Haroesis) at Kom Ombo. The temple at Kom Ombo is unusual, as it is dedicated to two gods.

A temple complex that still stands out from all the others is that of Ramesses II at Abu Simbel. The two temples there are unique because they were built purely for the glory of the king, not to glorify one of the gods.

Amun, Mut and Khonsu all had their own barques to carry them from Karnak to Luxor. This is Amun's barque.

 INTERNET LINK

Go to **www.usborne-quicklinks.com** *for links to Web sites where you can find out more about the history of the temples and festivals at Luxor and Karnak, illustrated with lots of photographs and maps.*

FESTIVALS OF AMUN

Amun had two major festivals a year – the Festival of Opet, shown here, and the Festival of the Valley, when the god was taken across the river to visit the tombs and mortuary temples on the west bank.

During the Festival of Opet, everyone gathered to see the magnificent procession as the gods made their way to Luxor.

Amun's statue was carried to his barque in another smaller barque.

RELIGION IN DAILY LIFE

In spite of the fact that they weren't allowed into the big temples, ordinary Egyptians lived and breathed religion. They believed that even the greatest of gods, such as Amun or Hathor, took a personal interest in their lives and in how they behaved. They were superstitous, and looked for deeper meanings in simple everyday events.

The lion-maned dwarf god Bes guarded children and the home.

CLOSE TO HOME

Temples were the homes of gods on Earth, so people would stand outside them to pray. But you didn't have to go to one of the major temples to worship. Each village had its own shrines to its chosen gods, including the major ones, where people could say prayers or make offerings. At shrines and temples, people often erected stones called *stelae*, with ears carved on them to remind the gods to listen to their prayers.

People's homes also had little shrines within them, often in niches in the wall. These would be dedicated to ancestors, or gods such as Bes and Tawaret who protected the home.

The goddess Tawaret was represented as a female hippopotamus. She was the goddess of pregnant women and childbirth.

SPEAKING TO THE GODS

The easiest way to discover the will of the gods was to get a scribe to write down a question. You then gave this to a priest, who would take it into the temple, where the god would answer it. This was known as 'consulting an oracle'. In fact, it was a priest who gave the answers, but he believed that he was inspired by the god. If a prayer was answered, people left a gift of thanks at the temple.

On feast days, when the god's statue was carried out on a barque by priests, people sang, knelt before it or dashed forward to ask it a question. The answer ('yes' or 'no') was shown by the movement of the barque. If the answer was 'yes', the statue would move forwards or back, or become suddenly heavy, forcing its carriers to their knees.

⬤ INTERNET LINK

At **www.usborne-quicklinks.com** there's a link to the **Cairo Museum's Animal Mummy Project Web site**, where you can learn more about sacred animals and Egyptian pets.

Some amulets, such as these golden lizards, were fitted into necklaces and bracelets.

Below are examples of other amulets. They were often based on hieroglyphs.

MAGIC, DREAMS AND OMENS

People believed that they were surrounded by the powers of good and evil. There were lucky days and unlucky days. Everyone wore good luck charms called amulets, and looked for omens to reveal the future or the gods' wishes. Dreams and signs such as shooting stars were seen as messages from the gods, and priests were asked to interpret them. People also turned to priest-magicians to ward off bad luck.

The funeral procession of the Apis bull led to the Serapeum at Saqqara.

SACRED ANIMALS

People believed that the gods could send their spirits to live in the creatures associated with them. By the Late Period, this applied to whole species – for example, the spirit of Bast was believed to live in every cat. When they died, these creatures were embalmed. Many were buried in animal cemeteries such as the one at Saqqara, where millions of mummified birds, cats, dogs and other animals have been found.

THE APIS BULL

The most important creatures buried at Saqqara were the Apis bulls. They were always black, with a white patch on their forehead and double white hairs in their tail. There was only one Apis bull at any one time. He lived in comfort with his mother in Ptah's temple in Memphis, and was paraded during religious festivals. When the bull died, he was mummified and taken to the Serapeum, a huge tomb underground. Then the search began for the new Apis bull.

The mummified bull was carried on a sacred barque.

These are examples of mummified animals – a cat, a dog or jackal, and a young calf.

DEATH AND THE AFTERLIFE

Death came all too soon to many Egyptians, often before the age of thirty. So it's hardly surprising that they had a strong belief in the 'Next World', where they would go to live. They spent a lot of time preparing for this and had a clear idea of what it would be like, what they would need and what would happen along the way.

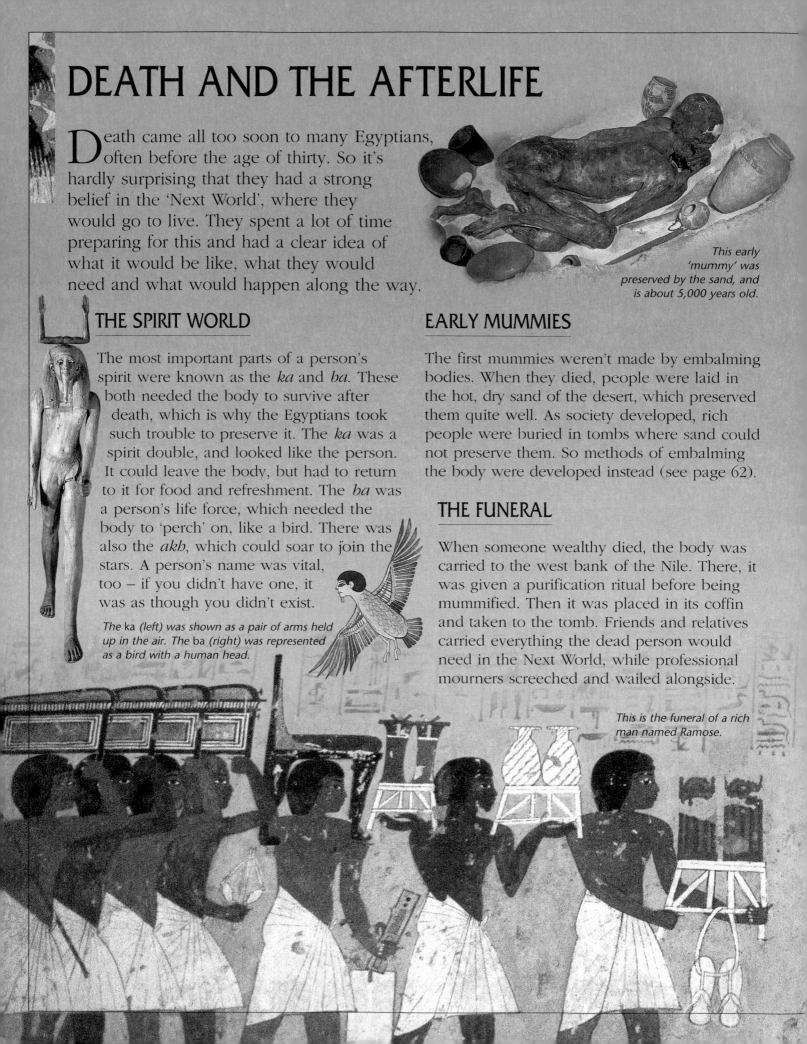

This early 'mummy' was preserved by the sand, and is about 5,000 years old.

THE SPIRIT WORLD

The most important parts of a person's spirit were known as the *ka* and *ba*. These both needed the body to survive after death, which is why the Egyptians took such trouble to preserve it. The *ka* was a spirit double, and looked like the person. It could leave the body, but had to return to it for food and refreshment. The *ba* was a person's life force, which needed the body to 'perch' on, like a bird. There was also the *akh*, which could soar to join the stars. A person's name was vital, too – if you didn't have one, it was as though you didn't exist.

The ka (left) was shown as a pair of arms held up in the air. The ba (right) was represented as a bird with a human head.

EARLY MUMMIES

The first mummies weren't made by embalming bodies. When they died, people were laid in the hot, dry sand of the desert, which preserved them quite well. As society developed, rich people were buried in tombs where sand could not preserve them. So methods of embalming the body were developed instead (see page 62).

THE FUNERAL

When someone wealthy died, the body was carried to the west bank of the Nile. There, it was given a purification ritual before being mummified. Then it was placed in its coffin and taken to the tomb. Friends and relatives carried everything the dead person would need in the Next World, while professional mourners screeched and wailed alongside.

This is the funeral of a rich man named Ramose.

THE OPENING OF THE MOUTH

At the tomb, the mummy was placed upright and a priest performed a ceremony called 'The Opening of the Mouth'. By touching the hands and feet, eyes, ears, nose and lips of the coffin, the priests 'freed' the senses so that they could function in the Next World. Then the coffin was placed in the tomb, surrounded by food, furniture and other necessities, and the tomb was sealed up.

Objects with symbolic meaning, called 'adzes', were used to touch the mummy during the Opening of the Mouth ceremony.

THE JOURNEY TO THE AFTERLIFE

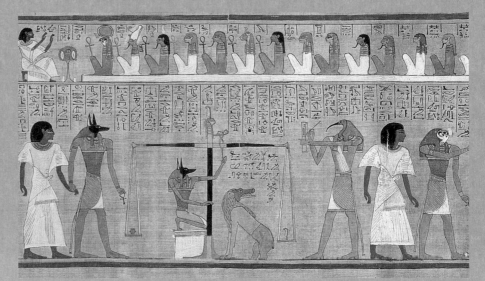

Anubis weighs the heart. Ammut waits hungrily next to him as Thoth writes down the verdict.

The journey to the Next World was a long and dangerous one for the person and their *ba*. First, this involved passing many gateways guarded by monsters to reach the place of judgement.

There, the person had to recite a long list of sins in front of 42 judges, and swear they had not committed any of them. The god Anubis would then take their heart and place it on the scales to be balanced against the feather of Ma'at, or truth, while Thoth stood by to write down the verdict. If the person had led a good life, their heart would be as light as the feather, and they would pass on to meet Osiris and their ancestors in the Next World. If the heart was heavy with sins, it would be eaten by a crocodile-headed monster called Ammut.

Professional mourners wailed and wept at Ramose's funeral.

EMBALMING AND MUMMIES

The embalming process, which prevented bodies from rotting away, was perfected over hundreds of years. If it was done properly, it was a lengthy, messy and gruesome job, but it did work.

Many New Kingdom mummies are still in amazingly good condition today. After the New Kingdom, standards waned, but bodies were still mummified until beyond the time of the Ptolemies.

THE NEW KINGDOM METHOD

Mummification took 70 days altogether. First, a slit was made in the side of the body so that the 'viscera' – the intestines, lungs, liver and stomach – could be taken out. The viscera were embalmed separately and placed in four 'canopic jars' (see opposite). The heart was left in the body, because Egyptians believed it would be judged in the Next World.

The body is cut open and the internal organs taken out.

Next, the embalmers covered the body with a salt called natron, a preservative that also soaked up the moisture. After about 35–40 days, the body was completely dried out. Then it was stuffed with materials soaked in oils and resins to make it a normal shape again, and the slit was sewn up.

Embalmers covering the body with natron

The body now had to be wrapped in layers of linen, starting with the fingers and toes.

Jewels and amulets (charms) were placed between the layers, to protect the person in the next life, and each layer was covered in oils, resins and perfumes, too.

The wrapping of the mummy is almost finished.

Finally, a mask was placed over the mummy's head. This was done by the chief embalmer, wearing the jackal mask of the embalming god Anubis. At last, the mummy was ready to be put in its coffin.

The chief embalmer says prayers over the completed mummy.

Over time, the oils and resins used in the wrapping stage became thick and sticky, almost like tar. The local word for this substance was *mumiya*, meaning 'bitumen' (tar is made partly of bitumen). So, this is where the word 'mummy' comes from.

Seti I's amazing mummy shows the effectiveness of the New Kingdom method of embalming.

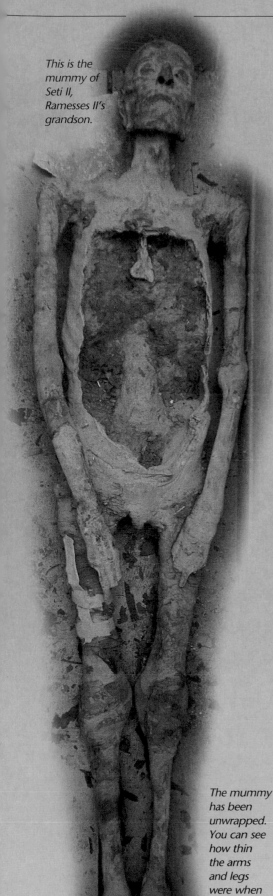

This is the mummy of Seti II, Ramesses II's grandson.

The mummy has been unwrapped. You can see how thin the arms and legs were when they were dried out.

CANOPIC JARS

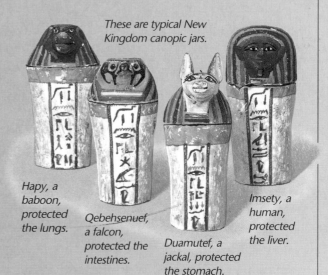

These are typical New Kingdom canopic jars.

There were usually four canopic jars with each mummy, containing the mummified liver, lungs, stomach and intestines. Each jar had a different stopper, in the form of one of the four sons of Horus, who protected the viscera.

Hapy, a baboon, protected the lungs.

Qebehsenuef, a falcon, protected the intestines.

Duamutef, a jackal, protected the stomach.

Imsety, a human, protected the liver.

MUMMIES REVEAL THEIR SECRETS

In the 19th century, mummies were often unwrapped so that investigators could inspect them. Later, it was recognized that this practice damaged them badly, so it was stopped. Now, when scientists want to find out about a mummy, they put it into a CAT scanner, which sees through all the bandages. They can also carry out tests on tiny scraps of mummy flesh to find out about their DNA, the unique blueprint that each of us has in our cells. For example, DNA tests have shown that Tutankhamun and the body found in KV55 (see page 28) were definitely related.

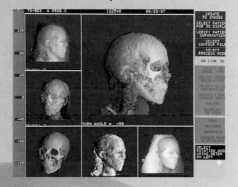

Modern technology: below, a wrapped mummy inside a CAT scanner. Right, images of mummies' faces, reconstructed by a computer.

COFFINS AND TOMBS

The coffins and tombs that mummies were placed in were as important as the embalming process itself. They were often lavishly decorated, and the decorations and inscriptions were a vital part of what the deceased person would need on the journey to the Next World.

*Sometimes, 'reserve heads' like this one of a princess, were placed in their owners' tombs to help the **ka** to recognize the body.*

COFFINS AND SARCOPHAGI

Anyone who was rich had their mummy placed in a coffin. In the Old and Middle Kingdoms, coffins were rectangular. They were brightly painted, with an *udjat* eye (see page 49) on the outside in the same position as the body's head, so that the dead person could see out. In the Middle Kingdom, people started making human-shaped coffins. An *udjat* eye wasn't needed, as the coffin had its own face, an idealized portrait of the person inside.

If you were royalty or very rich, you might have several coffins that nestled neatly inside each other. Sometimes these were placed in a big sarcophagus, an outer coffin made of stone. Coffins were usually rectangular, but in the Late Period some were human-shaped.

This is the tomb of Ramesses IV, with the king's sarcophagus in its burial chamber.

INSIDE A TOMB

Tombs were made in many shapes and sizes, from the brick mastabas of the early periods to the kings' amazing pyramids and rock-cut tombs. Tombs were only ever for the rich – the poor were buried in the sand.

All tombs had a burial chamber for the sarcophagus or coffin. Some had other chambers, too, such as 'chapels' where food could be left for the dead person's *ka* (see page 60). The burial chamber itself was sealed off, but the Egyptians believed that the *ka* would need to get in and out somehow. So a 'false door' was painted or carved on the inside, through which the *ka* could come and go.

This is a Late Period coffin. A portrait of the dead person is carved into the lid.

READY FOR THE NEXT LIFE

Egyptians believed that life after death would be very similar to life on earth. There would be work to do and houses to live in, so the dead person needed many of the things they used in life, such as food, clothes and furniture.

People obviously hoped, though, that the next life would be much better than the first – that harvests wouldn't fail, and that life would always be relaxed and enjoyable. But just in case they were required to do hard or difficult work, little figures called *ushabtis* were placed with the body. These were the dead person's servants, ready to obey orders and carry out whatever jobs needed doing.

Ushabtis were often placed in their own coffin or box, like these wooden New Kingdom ushabtis. The box is decorated with funerary scenes.

POWERFUL PAINTINGS

The paintings, writings and carvings on the walls of tombs weren't just for decoration. They were another part of what the person would need after death. For example, a scene of someone baking bread would ensure that the dead person knew how to do this in the Next World.

This wall painting in the tomb of Nakht shows a man rounding up his cattle.

TEXTS FOR GUIDANCE

Writings on the walls of tombs were there to guide the person on the difficult journey to the afterlife. In the Old Kingdom, kings had spells and prayers carved inside their pyramids. These writings became known as the Pyramid Texts. In the Middle Kingdom, ordinary people adapted these for their own coffins. These adaptations are known as the Coffin Texts.

In the New Kingdom, a whole new set of writings appeared, known as the *Book of the Dead*. There were five parts – the *Book of what is in the underworld*, the *Book of gates*, the *Book of caverns*, the *Book of earth* and the *Litany of Re*. Each dealt with an aspect of the afterlife – the *Book of gates*, for example, was for getting past the monsters guarding the twelve gates of the night.

 INTERNET LINK

At www.usborne-quicklinks.com there's a link to the British Museum Ancient Egypt Web site where you can take part in a "challenge" to get you through the underworld.

THE PYRAMIDS OF GIZA

The Great Pyramid of Khufu

Khafre's pyramid

Menkaure's pyramid

Even today, the pyramids of Khufu, Khafre and Menkaure at Giza seem mysterious and awe-inspiring – especially the biggest, Khufu's Great Pyramid. But Egyptologists have solved many of their mysteries. We now have a firm idea of both when they were built, and how.

THE GREAT PYRAMID

Until the 19th century, Khufu's Great Pyramid was the tallest building in the world. It was built in around 2550BC and is made of over 2 million blocks of limestone that were quarried nearby. Its proportions are perfectly symmetrical. Each side is 230m (755ft) wide at the bottom, and is aligned exactly with one of the points of the compass (north, south, east and west).

INTERNET LINK

At **www.usbornequicklinks.com** you'll find a link to a Web site where you can go on a virtual tour of the pyramids and find out lots of other information about them.

INSIDE KHUFU'S PYRAMID

The Egyptians never meant it to be easy to get inside the pyramid. They blocked the entrance with huge granite stones, and covered its entire surface with smooth limestone blocks. These blocks were placed together so closely that it was difficult to get even a knife blade in between them. Even so, robbers managed to break in, probably as early as the First Intermediate Period (c. 2150BC). By the time 19th-century explorers came along, the pyramid was empty – apart from a huge granite sarcophagus with no lid.

Three chambers have been found inside the pyramid, and a big hallway known as the Grand Gallery. From the King's Chamber, two small vents point upwards. One suggestion is that these were meant to line up with the stars that the king's spirit would visit in the afterlife. But, in fact, the vents don't reach as far as the open air.

Inside the Great Pyramid of Khufu

The Grand Gallery

Vents

The King's Chamber

The Queen's Chamber

Pyramid entrance

Underground chamber that was never finished

HOW DID THEY DO IT?

Each stone in the pyramid weighs about 2½ tonnes (tons). That's heavy. So to pull them up each new layer of the pyramid, the Egyptians used ramps, which were gradually built up as the pyramid grew.

The ramps would probably have looked like this.

Teams of men hauled the slabs of stone up the ramps with the help of rollers underneath.

The teams of men working on the pyramids were highly organized.

KHUFU THE TYRANT?

The Greek historian Herodotus claimed that Khufu used slaves to carry out his staggering task, but he got many facts wrong. Now, we know the Egyptians took great pride in building the pyramids. Skilled craftsmen were employed full time, but most workers were peasants doing their work tax, or 'corvee' (see page 42).

KHAFRE AND MENKAURE

Khafre's pyramid is similar to Khufu's. It is not quite as big, but it looks bigger because it was built on higher ground. You can still see some of its outer limestone casing at the top.

Menkaure's pyramid is smaller than the other two but it would have been difficult to build, as its outer casing was of granite. Granite is harder to cut than limestone, and also had to be transported all the way from Aswan in Upper Egypt.

A BUSTLING AREA

Photographs of the pyramids often give the impression that they sit isolated in the desert, but in ancient times, they were surrounded by palaces, temples and other tombs, and there were ports that bustled with boats. Priests and other workers lived close by in busy towns – a recent discovery has been the bakery where the workers' bread was baked. In 1954, some pits were discovered that held the kings' boats or 'barques'. Two boats had survived, including one belonging to King Khufu himself (see page 72).

Overseers made sure the job was done properly.

Each stone was placed in position very carefully.

Accidents were common, but doctors were always available to treat broken bones.

Water carriers supplied plenty of water for thirsty workers.

The rollers underneath the stones made the work a lot easier.

The ramp was made of sand and rubble.

The ramp was probably held in place by a mud-brick wall.

BURIED IN THE ROCKS

Some noblemen had used tombs cut out of rocks from the end of the Old Kingdom. For kings, though, tombs like this didn't replace pyramids until the New Kingdom. Most of the New Kingdom pharaohs were buried in tombs in the Valley of the Kings, opposite Thebes. Some queens were buried there too, but later queens had their own burial valley. Many nobles were buried nearby as well.

VALLEY OF THE KINGS

The Valley of the Kings is set among dramatic limestone cliffs, and the tombs are tucked between folds in the rock. Although they were not as visible as pyramids, most people knew where they were, so they were constantly guarded by the Medjay (police). Even so, by the end of the New Kingdom, most of them had been robbed.

The tombs are decorated with scenes from the *Book of the Dead*. Scenes from everyday life weren't generally shown, because kings wouldn't be expected to do any normal jobs in the next life.

TOMB LAYOUT

The tombs vary in size and shape, but they all have steps and corridors leading deep into the rock. The older, 18th dynasty tombs (such as Tutankhamun's) were built in an L-shape. Later, they had long corridors with annexes leading off and a burial chamber at the end. One example is the magnificent tomb of Seti I.

Burial chambers

Plans of the tombs of Tutankhamun (top left) and Seti I (right). The layouts are not to scale – Seti's is actually much, much bigger than Tutankhamun's.

In this overhead view of the Valley of the Kings, you can see how the tombs are tucked into niches in the cliffs.

Tuthmosis III
Seti II
Tuthmosis I

Amenhotep II
Ramesses III
Horemheb
Ramesses VI
Tutankhamun
Merenptah

Ramesses I
Seti I

Ramesses II

HOW THEY WERE MADE

First of all, a tomb's basic shape was cut out of the rock by stonecutters. Then plasterers applied a layer of fine, smooth plaster to the inside walls. Next, a draftsman drew a grid and outlines of the scene in red, using strict rules of proportion (see page 55). Any corrections were made in black. Then painters came along to fill in the details.

When the rock was hard enough, the tombs had sunken reliefs instead of flat paintings. In this case, the carvers did their job once the draftsmen had finished.

The reliefs in Horemheb's tomb were never finished, so you can still see the draftsman's grid and drawings followed by the carvers.

NEARBY TOMBS

South of the Valley of the Kings, scattered among the cliffs facing the Nile, lie the tombs of nobles. They are decorated with religious scenes, both of the owner's funeral and the life the nobles hoped for after death. There are also beautiful tombs at Deir el Medina, made by the workers for their own use.

NEFERTARI'S TOMB

A little further south of the nobles' tombs lies the Valley of the Queens, where there are tombs of some of the royal children as well as queens. The most beautiful of these tombs belongs to Nefertari, the chief queen of Ramesses II. Many people think it is the most beautiful royal tomb in all ancient Egypt. It has recently been carefully restored to its former brilliance, and a few people are allowed in to see it every day.

This is an image of Nefertari from the walls of her tomb.

The paintings in Nefertari's tomb are amazingly vivid and bright.

Inside the tomb of Pashedu, one of the workers from the village of Deir el Medina

Many of the paintings of Nefertari show her wearing very fine white linen that is almost see-through.

MORTUARY TEMPLES

As well as cult temples, many of the temples still standing today are the New Kingdom 'mortuary' temples. These were built for the worship of kings after their death. Unlike cult temples, mortuary temples were built on the west bank of the Nile, the kingdom of the dead.

A CLUSTER OF TEMPLES

Most mortuary temples were built near the Valley of the Kings at Thebes. Many are now just ruins, but the picture below gives an artist's reconstruction of where they once stood. You can also see where the Valley of the Kings, the Valley of the Queens and the workmen's village of Deir el Medina are situated.

THE COLOSSI OF MEMNON

These two statues once stood in front of Amenhotep III's mortuary temple, which was dismantled by later kings for its stone.

Some time after Amenhotep's temple was dismantled, an earthquake cracked one of the remaining two statues. After this, it began to make a strange noise at dawn. The Greeks thought the sound was the sighing of Memnon, one of their heroes who was killed in battle. In fact, it was probably an effect of the rising sun's heat on air and moisture trapped in the crack in the stone. In 199AD, the Roman emperor Septimus Severus sealed the crack – and the moaning 'Colossus of Memnon' has been silent ever since.

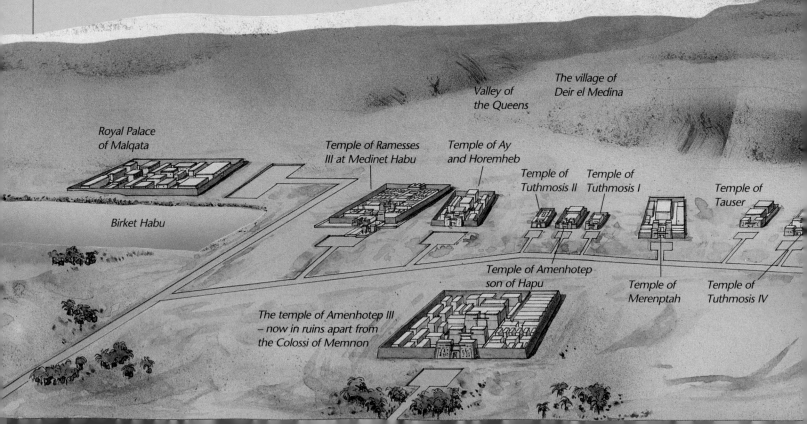

Royal Palace
of Malqata

Birket Habu

Temple of Ramesses
III at Medinet Habu

Temple of Ay
and Horemheb

Valley of
the Queens

The village of
Deir el Medina

Temple of
Tuthmosis II

Temple of
Tuthmosis I

Temple of
Tauser

Temple of Amenhotep
son of Hapu

Temple of
Merenptah

Temple of
Tuthmosis IV

The temple of Amenhotep III
– now in ruins apart from
the Colossi of Memnon

Ramesses III's massive temple at Medinet Habu is still in good condition.

THE TEMPLES AT ABYDOS

Abydos, halfway between Memphis and Thebes, was Egypt's most holy place. This was because Osiris, the god of the dead, was said to be buried there. It was therefore the ideal place for anyone else to be buried, too, and became a place of pilgrimage.

In the 19th Dynasty, Seti I built a beautiful mortuary temple at Abydos. It is now one of the most beautiful temples still standing in Egypt, because much of its paintwork has been preserved. It is also unique in that it has seven chapels dedicated to different gods. Seti's son Ramesses II completed it, and built another temple of his own there, too.

THE RAMESSEUM

Like everything that Ramesses II built, his mortuary temple, known as the Ramesseum, is on a huge scale. It included a massive statue of Ramesses himself, about 20m (60ft) high. Now, the statue has toppled over, and its broken remains inspired a poem by an English poet, Shelley. This poem, *Ozymandias*, mocks Ramesses for his arrogance and delusions of grandeur.

MEDINET HABU

Not to be outdone by his predecessor, Ramesses III also built an enormous mortuary temple. It is carved with many battle scenes, showing Ramesses' success in battle against the Libyans and the Sea Peoples. Some scenes are gruesome, showing scribes counting piles of chopped-off hands to calculate how many enemies had been killed.

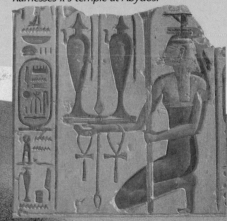

Beautiful sunken reliefs can still be seen on Ramesses II's temple at Abydos.

Valley of the Kings (hidden behind the mountain)

Deir el Bahri

Tombs of the nobles

Temple of Siptah

Temple of Tuthmosis III

Temple of Mentuhotep II (Middle Kingdom)

Temple of Hatshepsut

The Ramesseum, Ramesses II's temple

INTERNET LINK

At **www.usborne-quicklinks.com** you'll find a link to the **Theban Mapping Project Web site**, which has more details, photographs and plans of mortuary temples.

Temple of Seti I

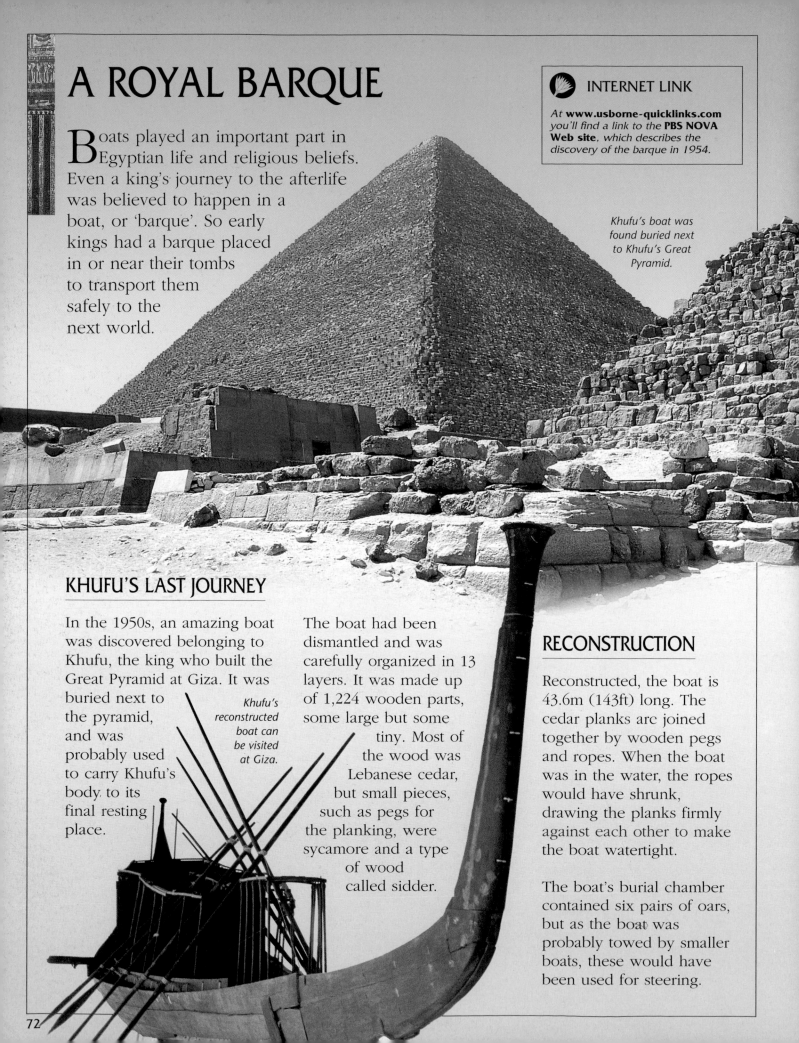

A ROYAL BARQUE

Boats played an important part in Egyptian life and religious beliefs. Even a king's journey to the afterlife was believed to happen in a boat, or 'barque'. So early kings had a barque placed in or near their tombs to transport them safely to the next world.

INTERNET LINK

At www.usborne-quicklinks.com you'll find a link to the PBS NOVA Web site, which describes the discovery of the barque in 1954.

Khufu's boat was found buried next to Khufu's Great Pyramid.

KHUFU'S LAST JOURNEY

In the 1950s, an amazing boat was discovered belonging to Khufu, the king who built the Great Pyramid at Giza. It was buried next to the pyramid, and was probably used to carry Khufu's body to its final resting place.

Khufu's reconstructed boat can be visited at Giza.

The boat had been dismantled and was carefully organized in 13 layers. It was made up of 1,224 wooden parts, some large but some tiny. Most of the wood was Lebanese cedar, but small pieces, such as pegs for the planking, were sycamore and a type of wood called sidder.

RECONSTRUCTION

Reconstructed, the boat is 43.6m (143ft) long. The cedar planks are joined together by wooden pegs and ropes. When the boat was in the water, the ropes would have shrunk, drawing the planks firmly against each other to make the boat watertight.

The boat's burial chamber contained six pairs of oars, but as the boat was probably towed by smaller boats, these would have been used for steering.

EVERYDAY LIFE

HOUSES AND HOMES

The very earliest Egyptian houses were made from wooden posts and bundles of reeds. By the time the country was unified, mud brick was used instead. From then on, everyone – rich or poor – lived in mud-brick houses. The difference lay in how big they were, their facilities and how they were decorated. Kings' palaces were big and luxurious, but poor people's houses could be very cramped indeed.

THE PROBLEM WITH MUD

There was never a shortage of mud in Egypt. The annual Nile flood provided plenty of it, but it also meant that houses had to be built on higher ground. Space was limited, so houses were rebuilt on the same site. As a result, not many original houses have survived, but some foundations have been discovered. Whole workmen's villages have been excavated at Karun, near the Faiyum; Deir el Medina, near the Valley of the Kings; and at Tell el Amarna, Akhenaten's abandoned city.

WORKERS' COTTAGES

The village at Deir el Medina was founded in about 1550BC for the craftsmen and artists who were building the royal tombs (see pages 68 and 80). It thrived for about 500 years. This village has given us a good idea of how many people lived in the New Kingdom.

The village had one long central street running north to south. It was narrow and airless. The houses themselves, built on either side of the street, were long and narrow, and most had four small rooms in them. About 60 families lived in the village at any one time.

A typical scene in the craftsmens' village of Deir el Medina. Some of the walls have been cut away so that you can see inside the houses.

People spent a lot of time on the roof, and slept there in hot weather.

The second room had a roof supported by one wooden column on a stone base. This was the living room.

The front room opened directly onto the street. This is where a lot of the household work was done.

Courtyard where the cooking was done

Wine cellar

Oven

The third room was often divided into two small rooms, one serving as a bedroom and the other as a storage room.

TOWN HOUSES

Because building land in ancient Egypt was so scarce, houses in towns were built tall and close together. Some were up to four floors high. The streets below were narrow and crowded. There was no public refuse or sewage system, and each household had to dispose of its own waste – in pits, the river, or simply by throwing it into the street. People spent as much time as possible on the roofs to catch the cool breezes, and to get away from the smell of the streets below.

A model of an Egyptian town house, showing several floors.

FURNITURE

Wooden furniture was very expensive, so most houses were very simply furnished. Tables, chairs and beds were usually made from cheap local wood or even reeds.

Rich households, though, had furniture made of expensive imported woods such as ebony and cedar, inlaid with ivory, precious metals, semi-precious stones and a kind of glass called faience. Sometimes it was even covered with gold.

Houses were lit by small oil-burning lamps. These were simply bowls with linseed oil and a wick (a piece of twisted cloth) inside them.

This chair belonged to a queen, so it is much more elaborate than the chairs owned by poorer people. The basic design, however, would have been the same.

⬤ INTERNET LINK

Go to **www.usborne-quicklinks.com** *for a link to a Web site where you can find photographs of Egyptian paintings and models, showing all kinds of houses and furniture and scenes from daily life.*

HOMES OF THE RICH

Rich people lived in luxurious villas. These villas had many different rooms, and a big hall in the middle for entertaining guests. Both the inside and outside walls were plastered and painted. These villas often had lovely gardens, too, with shady trees and pools.

This wall painting is in a tomb at Thebes that belonged to a rich man called Nakht. Here, Nakht is shown with his wife in the garden.

Nakht's house had vents in the roof to keep the house cool, and was built on a platform, to keep the rooms dry.

WOMEN AND FAMILY LIFE

Egyptian society revolved around the family, and the main role of women was to run the family household and have children. Most did not have jobs or go out to work. But compared with women in other ancient civilizations, women in ancient Egypt had quite a lot of freedom, and many of the same rights as men.

Wealthy women had elaborate burials, just as men did. This carved image of a woman forms part of a sarcophagus lid from the Late Period.

WOMEN IN SOCIETY

Women did not have completely equal status with men in ancient Egypt, and most ordinary women couldn't read or write. But any woman was entitled to carry out business deals and contracts, own property, or be a witness in court.

Upper and middle class women were generally better educated and many of them could read and write. They couldn't hold important jobs such as government posts, but they often helped their husbands with their work.

Wall paintings show women musicians and dancers.

HAVING A JOB

Although most women stayed at home, some did have careers. Noblewomen could become courtiers or priestesses, while other women could become singers, dancers, musicians and acrobats at the royal court and in temples. There were also women weavers, gardeners, professional mourners and even a few doctors. Poorer women often worked as servants and nannies for royal or rich families. Sometimes, this brought them power and influence – the sons of some royal nannies held important positions at court.

If a woman's husband was absent for some reason, this gave her the opportunity to run the family business. Some women ran whole farms.

Here, a New Kingdom landowner checks up on the workers on her estate.

GETTING MARRIED

Kings had several wives, but most men had only one. Men married at about twenty, but girls married earlier – some as young as fourteen. People's husbands and wives were chosen for them by their parents – usually someone from the same background, or the same family. Even so, statues, paintings and love poems show that they often loved each other very much.

A statue of the king Akhenaten, holding hands with his chief queen, Nefertiti.

MARRIED LIFE

A couple's marriage was a legal settlement made up of financial arrangements. A husband gave his wife an allowance to live on and run the household, but both husband and wife could own property separately. The couple also set up a joint fund, the husband putting in two-thirds and the wife one-third. This served as a nest-egg for their children.

If a marriage wasn't a happy one, a couple could get divorced simply by making a statement in front of witnesses. Most people tried to avoid this, though – relatives of the couple would try to persuade them to resolve their differences. If a divorce was unavoidable, children stayed with the mother, and both parents were free to marry again.

INTERNET LINK

At **www.usborne-quicklinks.com** *you'll find a link to the* **British Museum's Ancient Egypt Web site**, *which will take you through a day in the life of a farmer's family and a nobleman's family.*

SONS AND DAUGHTERS

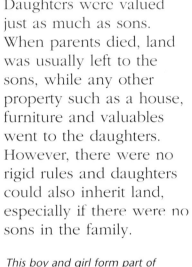

The Egyptians made plenty of toys for children to play with. These are clay balls, and a toy dog with a handle that opens its mouth.

Daughters were valued just as much as sons. When parents died, land was usually left to the sons, while any other property such as a house, furniture and valuables went to the daughters. However, there were no rigid rules and daughters could also inherit land, especially if there were no sons in the family.

This boy and girl form part of a 5th dynasty sculpture of a family group.

THE FARMING LIFE

Farming formed the backbone of Egyptian society. The farmland along the Nile was rich and fertile, so farmers were able to grow far more than they could eat. Some of the extra grain was paid in taxes to the king, who used it to pay servants, finance building projects, or exported it.

This picture shows a 'shaduf' for lifting water, like the ones used in ancient Egypt.

LIFE-GIVING WATER

The farming calendar was based around the rise and fall of the river Nile. Every spring, rain and melted snow from the mountains of Ethiopia swelled the river. Sometime around July, the Nile overflowed its banks, flooding the whole valley. This was known as the Inundation.

There was a lot hanging on the level of the flood. If it was too low, there could be a poor harvest and famine. If it was too high, it flooded villages and sometimes washed them away.

IRRIGATION SYSTEMS

The Egyptians learned to make the most of the Inundation as far back as Predynastic times. The land was divided into fields, with irrigation canals between them. The government used corvée workers (see page 42) to repair the canals properly every year.

People still had to carry water in jars to areas not reached by the Inundation – a heavy, time-consuming job. From the New Kingdom onwards, lifting the water was made slightly easier by devices called shadufs (see above).

AFTER THE FLOOD

By the end of October, the waters had ebbed away, leaving behind a thick layer of fertile mud called silt. Farmers now had to work the fields and sow the seeds. The major crops were wheat and barley, for making bread and beer. After sowing, a herd of sheep was often driven over the ground, so that the seeds were buried and trampled into the soil.

Today, farmers still rely on the Nile to water their crops.

An Old Kingdom painting of geese. These birds were kept by farmers for their meat and eggs.

HARVEST TIME

Once the crop was ripe (sometime between March and June), everyone piled in to harvest it with sickles. Sometimes the army was called in to help. It was vital to finish before the summer heat set in, so that the irrigation ditches could be repaired before the next flood.

The grain was loaded onto donkeys and taken to the threshing floor. Threshing means separating the grain from the stalk, and this was done by cows or donkeys trampling over the crop. Then the grain was 'winnowed' – thrown into the air for the wind to blow away the pieces of straw and chaff.

Tomb painting showing the grain being winnowed

Finally, a tenth of the crop had to be handed over to the king in taxes. The peasants usually had to give a portion to their landlord, too.

MEAT AND MILK

Most land was used to grow crops, rather than for grazing animals. But sheep, goats and pigs could survive anywhere, so all farmers kept a few, along with geese, ducks and pigeons. Beef was a luxury – only rich people kept cattle for their meat and milk.

PLENTY OF VARIETY

Although grain was the most common crop, many farmers grew flax, for making linen. They also grew a wide range of vegetables and fruit, including beans, lentils, onions, garlic, lettuce, cucumbers, leeks, melons, grapes, pomegranates, dates and figs.

SKILLED CRAFTSMEN

The craftsmen of ancient Egypt were well-paid and highly respected members of the community. Although the tools and techniques available to them were very simple, the quality of their work was incredibly high, and much of it has survived to amaze us today.

PLENTIFUL WORK

Most craftsmen worked for the king, on the magnificent tomb and temple projects or on the palace and temple finery. Some nobles could afford to have workshops, too. Craftsmen also increased their income by taking on private work in their spare time.

DEIR EL MEDINA

We know a lot about craftsmen's lives from the village of Deir el Medina, home to the men who built the tombs in the Valley of the Kings. They were wealthier than average craftsmen, with enough leisure time to make beautiful tombs for themselves as well as the kings. They also had fun using their skills at home, doodling on ostraca (limestone flakes).

This unshaven stonemason was quickly sketched on an ostracon by another worker at Deir el Medina.

The craftsmen weren't paid in money, but in grain, fish, vegetables, meat, salt, beer and oil, with occasional 'extras' such as silver and wine. They were given so much grain that they could trade some of it for other goods. The village was in the desert, so they had people to bring them water, and they were also given slave girls to grind their grain.

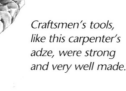

Craftsmen's tools, like this carpenter's adze, were strong and very well made.

AT THE TOMBS

The craftsmen stayed in huts in the Valley of the Kings while they worked on a tomb. They did an eight-hour day with a long midday break, and had a day off every ten days. They also had time off for the many religious festivals.

The men worked in two groups, one on each side of a tomb, with a foreman in charge of each group. A scribe kept records of materials and tools, the men's attendance and wages. Two other men looked after the storerooms.

A Middle Kingdom model of a carpenters' workshop

DIFFERENT SKILLS

A huge range of work was done by craftsmen using many different methods and materials. Here are just a few examples.

- Carpenters used different woods – local sycamore, fig and palm wood as well as imported ebony and cedar – to make statues and furniture.

- Metalsmiths and jewellers worked in copper, bronze, silver, gold and electrum (a mixture of gold and silver), which they hammered into shape. Metalsmiths also made models and statues by casting metal – melting it and pouring it into stone or pottery shapes.

- Potters worked with clay, or carved pots from the beautiful stones found in the desert. Some pots were decorated with a glaze such as faience, which looked rather like glass.

- Glassworkers made vessels by making a pot shape out of clay and sand. This shape was then dipped into a bowl of melted glass. When the glass cooled, the clay was scraped out.

Craftsmen working with gold in their workshop

IN A WORKSHOP

Wall paintings show that other craftsmen generally worked together in workshops. As in the tombs, the workers were closely supervised by foremen who made sure that the finished products reached the highest standards, and scribes kept track of everything. The foremen were also in charge of the strict security system, especially where craftsmen worked with gold, silver or precious stones.

⬕ INTERNET LINK

At **www.usborne-quicklinks. com** you'll find a link to the **British Museum Ancient Egypt Web site**, where you can read more about craftsmen's lives and explore different workshops.

This relief shows a metalworker blowing into a furnace. This was hot, difficult work that would have been dangerous, too.

JOBS FOR ALL

There were a number of things that Egyptian society really couldn't do without. These included bread, oil and beer, linen, which everyone wore, and mud bricks, which everyone built their houses with. Making these may not have been the most skilled or respected work, but it kept a lot of people very busy.

This wall painting from the tomb of Khaemwese shows the different processes involved in making wine.

BAKING BREAD

Whether you were rich or poor in ancient Egypt, bread was an important part of your diet. Loaves came in all shapes and sizes, and the types of flour varied, too. Richer people ate white bread, but most people ate a coarser brown version. Sweet pastries were popular, often made into fancy shapes.

Bread was made by adding water to flour to make dough. Most of it was made in the home by women and servants. On building projects, though, large amounts of bread were made on site for the workers to eat.

In this Middle Kingdom model, the figure on the left is making beer.

DRINKS ALL ROUND

The most popular drink in Egypt was beer. Grain and bread were soaked in water, then mashed, put through a sieve and left to ferment. Sometimes things such as spices and dates were added to the beer, then it was sieved again. It was stored in large pottery jars sealed with clay stoppers, but it had to be drunk soon after it was made as it went flat quickly.

Richer people also drank wine. The grapes were grown on trellises and taken for pressing as soon as they were ripe. Then they were trampled underfoot, and finally the juice was poured into pottery jars to ferment into wine.

The two right-hand figures are kneading dough to make bread.

PRECIOUS REEDS

The reeds that grew along the Nile had many uses. They were chopped and used to make boats and roofs; and they were dried and woven to make baskets, mats, chests and sandals. One special reed called papyrus was also used to make the precious papyrus scrolls used by scribes.

Papryus plant

To make paper, the outer skin was peeled away.

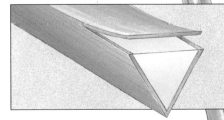

The pith was cut into strips and soaked.

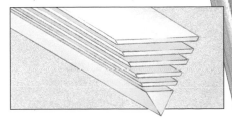

The strips were arranged on top of each other, hammered and pressed together with weights.

MAKING LINEN

Linen, made from the flax plant, varied from very coarse, rough cloth to the finest 'royal linen', which was so fine it was almost transparent. Only highly skilled workers made royal linen.

When the stalks of flax were harvested they were first soaked in water, then beaten. The strands were separated out with a comb and dried, then sticks called spindles were used to spin them into long threads. Finally, the threads were woven into cloth on looms.

These samples of ancient Egyptian linen were found at the craftsmen's village of Deir el Medina.

 INTERNET LINK

Go to **www.usborne-quicklinks.com** for a link to a Web site where you can find out about how papyrus changed Egyptian society, as well as more on how paper and linen were made.

MUD, GLORIOUS MUD

Most building work was done with mud bricks, not stone. Sand and chopped-up straw were added to mud to help bind it together. Then this was made into brick shapes, which were left to dry in the sun for a few days. And that was it – the bricks were ready to use.

SERVANTS AND SLAVES

Before the New Kingdom, there weren't many slaves in Egypt, though rich people had servants to do the chores and wait upon guests. But, when Egypt became a powerful empire, many prisoners of war were captured and slavery became very common. Even ordinary people like craftsmen had slaves.

Life as a slave varied. If you worked in a quarry or a building site, it was tough. But some slaves worked for kind people and were well treated. Some were set free, and a few even married into local families.

A servant carrying his master's belongings

THE EDUCATED FEW

Although most people couldn't read and write, Egyptian society was based on written records, so if you could write you were never short of work. The life of a scribe, or writer, was probably envied by other people – you didn't have to toil under the hot sun, and you were highly regarded in society, too.

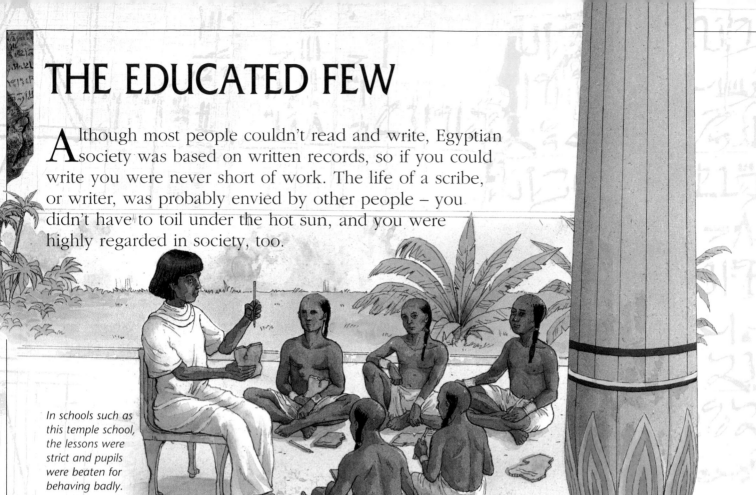

In schools such as this temple school, the lessons were strict and pupils were beaten for behaving badly.

WHO WENT TO SCHOOL?

Anyone could pay to go to school, so having an education depended on whether you could afford it. Peasants did their best to educate their sons, as this was the only way to improve their lot in life. Girls from poor families were rarely educated, but in rich families they learned to read and write like boys.

There were several kinds of schools. If you were from a noble family, you might be educated in the palace with the royal children. Next down were temple schools. There were village schools, too, attached to local shrines.

IN THE CLASSROOM

Boys started school aged about five, and learned both the hieroglyphic and hieratic scripts (see pages 86-87). They spent a lot of time copying and reciting texts to perfect their writing and reading skills. To teach younger pupils, teachers used a book called *Kemyt*, which means 'completion'. This was a very simple text of model letters,

There were plenty of these limestone flakes called 'ostraca' for pupils to write on.

phrases and expressions. Older students studied more advanced books. These were often classics of Egyptian literature, such as the *Books of Wisdom*, which gave advice to young men about how to behave. Other texts talked about how wonderful it was to be a scribe rather than a craftsman, which must have given scribes a big sense of their own importance.

 INTERNET LINK

At **www.usborne-quicklinks.com** *you'll find a link to a Web site where you can find out how hieroglyphs work, and learn about the ancient Egyptian counting system, too.*

THE NEXT STEP

Once a pupil had mastered the basic arts of reading and writing, he could become a scribe. Many never went beyond this position. If you could afford it, though, you might go on to further studies, which could include mathematics, history, literature, religion, geography, languages, surveying, engineering, astronomy, medicine or accounting.

The Rhind Mathematical Papyrus describes different practical and mathematical problems and how to solve them.

THE BUSY SCRIBE

Even if you never progressed from being a scribe, there was always plenty of work to do composing letters or legal documents such as wills, marriages and business deals. Scribes also copied out documents in temple libraries, or wrote down questions for people who wanted to ask a god for advice.

There were scribes in every government department. If you were clever and had good connections, you could better yourself. If you kept tax and legal records, or worked in the foreign office, you might be able to become an adviser or even, eventually, a minister.

A seated scribe holds a papyrus in his lap, preparing to read it.

TOOLS OF THE TRADE

Important documents were written on papyrus (see page 83), the first kind of paper in the world. This was expensive, so unimportant writing was done on wooden tablets coated with plaster that could be wiped clean, or on pieces of broken limestone known as ostraca. There were two kinds of ink: black and red. These were stored in dry blocks on little palettes, and were moistened with water. Pens were made of reeds, and were rather like paintbrushes.

A scribe's ink palette. His equipment also included a little pot of water for moistening the ink.

Blocks of red and black ink

Reed pens

WRITING OF THE GODS

The ancient Egyptian language was written down in two ways. The picture writing you see carved on monuments is known as the hieroglyphic script. But there was also a simplified version, known as hieratic, which was easier and faster to write on papyrus.

THE HOLY SCRIPT

The Egyptians believed that writing had been given to them by Thoth, the god of wisdom. They called the script *mdw nṯr*, which means 'the words of the god'. They thought that the signs had a magic power of their own and could come to life.

Later, the Greeks called the script *hieroglyphs*, which means 'sacred sculptures'. This was because hieroglyphs were usually sculpted onto stone or painted onto the walls of tombs, not written down on papyrus.

HOW HIEROGLYPHS WORK

The hieroglyphic script is a very complex system of more than 700 pictures. Below are some of the simpler ways in which they work.

Many of the pictures stand for an actual object. When this is the case, there is often a small stroke near to it to confirm this.

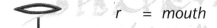

r = mouth

But as well as an object, each picture may represent a sound. It can appear in a word as just this sound, and not as the actual object. There are only 24 pictures that represent a single letter-sound.

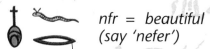

nfr = beautiful
(say 'nefer')

Here, this means 'r', not 'mouth'

Many of the other signs represent more than one letter and sound, or have some other meaning.

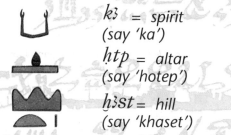

kꜣ = spirit
(say 'ka')

ḥtp = altar
(say 'hotep')

ḫꜣst = hill
(say 'khaset')

Often, it was difficult to tell what a word meant from just the 'letter' signs, so another sign was added at the end of the word to show what kind of word it was. These signs are called 'determinatives'.

ḫpi = to walk
(say 'khepi')

Determinatives

mi iw = cat
(say 'mioow')

The signs on the left:

ꜣ
i
y
ꜥ
w
b
p
f
m
n
r
h
ḥ
ḫ
ẖ
š
s
ḳ
k
g
t
ṯ
d
ḏ

These are the 24 signs that represent a single letter-sound.

Hieroglyphs carved on the walls of a tomb in the Valley of the Queens, with the paint still visible

ADDING THE VOWELS

The hieroglyphic 'letters' didn't include vowels, although there were a few semi-vowels, such as 'y'. The vowels sounds only appeared in the spoken language. This might seem odd, but there are still many languages like this (modern Arabic is one). In the case of ancient Egyptian, though, we are still not entirely sure how it sounded, so we have to guess at the vowel sounds, too. This is why you may see Egyptian words written differently in different books.

READING HIEROGLYPHS

It takes a long time to learn to read hieroglyphs properly. A good place to start, though, is to learn some of the kings' and queens' names. They are easy to spot because they are written in an oval frame that we call a 'cartouche'. This was there to give protection to the royal name.

Hieroglyphs can be read from left to right, right to left, or top to bottom. You can tell which way to read from symbols such as people and birds, which always face the beginning of the sentence. Here are some examples:

This reads from left to right and says 'Son of Re, Lord of Appearances, Seti beloved of Ptah'.

These are the same as the hieroglyphs above but are read from right to left.

These hieroglyphs are read from right to left and top to bottom. The right-hand column says, 'King of Upper and Lower Egypt, Lord of the Two Lands, User-Kheperu-Re beloved of Amun'.

HIERATIC AND DEMOTIC

The hieratic script, a kind of shorthand, developed in the Old Kingdom. The Greeks gave it this name, which means 'priestly', because it was mostly priests who used it. Then, during the Late Period (about 700BC), a new shorthand developed, simpler than either hieratic or heiroglyphics.

An example of the hieratic script

An example of the demotic script

Because it was easier to write, this script became known as demotic, which means 'the people's'.

WHAT HAPPENED NEXT?

After the fall of the Ptolemies, Egyptian culture began to decline as Christianity took over as the main religion. The Egyptian language began to change, because it was difficult to describe Christian beliefs with it.

This new Christian language was called Coptic, and Egyptian Christians are called Copts even today. In fact, the language used in Coptic churches is the closest language in the world to ancient Egyptian.

A temple pillar intricately carved with hieroglyphs

FEASTING AND FUN

The Egyptians loved having fun. This is clear from their tombs, which show scenes of banquets, making merry, and leisure pursuits such as hunting. These pictures were there to ensure that the dead person had a good time in the afterlife, but they show the Egyptians knew how to enjoy themselves while they were alive, too.

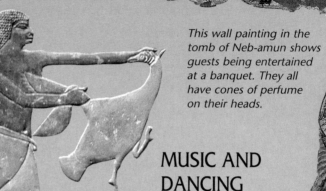

EXTRAVAGANT PARTIES

Rich Egyptians would often throw elaborate parties for their friends. They provided huge amounts of meat, vegetables and fruit, not to mention wine and beer. The dining area was decorated with flowers and bowls of fruit, and the best plates and cups were taken out of storage.

Guests were welcomed with a garland of flowers and taken to wash their hands in basins filled with scented water. Then they sat down on cushions, stools or chairs and had their first cup of wine. A servant went around the room and placed a small cone of perfumed ointment on everyone's heads. As things got going, the ointment melted and dripped down their wigs, keeping the guests cool and sweet-smelling.

Then the feasting began. People didn't do things in moderation. They ate and drank far too much and thoroughly enjoyed themselves.

A servant carries a goose to be slaughtered.

This wall painting in the tomb of Neb-amun shows guests being entertained at a banquet. They all have cones of perfume on their heads.

MUSIC AND DANCING

As well as good food and wine, the best parties always had lively entertainment. As the guests arrived, and throughout the meal, musicians played on harps and lyres, flutes, pipes and drums. When the food was finished, it was the turn of the singers and storytellers, dancers, acrobats and jugglers to perform.

Here, a flute player and a singer provide entertainment at a party.

Food would have been served on bowls such as this 18th dynasty faience bowl.

 INTERNET LINK

At **www.usborne-quicklinks.com** you'll find a link to the **British Museum's Ancient Egypt Web site**, where you can find out how to play the Egyptian game Senet, according to the most likely rules.

EXOTIC ANIMALS

Wild animals provided more sport for noblemen. Those who could afford it went hunting in the desert for hares, foxes, antelopes, ostriches and sometimes lions. At first this took place on foot, but in the New Kingdom they usually went in horse-drawn chariots. The hunt served as another excuse to have a party, with picnics, drinking and more fun.

RELAXING AT HOME

In contrast to their livelier leisure activities, the Egyptians also enjoyed sitting around playing board games. The most common game was called senet, a board game played with different pieces. This was played by everyone, from the royal family to farmers.

The ancient rules for playing senet have been lost, but the most likely rules have now been established.

THE SPORTING LIFE

Hunting and fishing were vital for many Egyptians, but richer people hunted simply for sport. The most dangerous sport was hunting crocodiles and hippos. A team of hunters harpooned the animals, then dragged them ashore with ropes and nets.

Mainly, though, noblemen went hunting for birds, accompanied by their servants. They took their pet cats, too, which were trained to flush out the game. The noblemen used specially-shaped throwing sticks, which could easily break a bird's neck.

Throwing sticks were used to break birds' necks.

Wall paintings show the Egyptians' interest in different birds and animals.

ALL DRESSED UP

The Egyptians went to a lot of trouble over their appearance, but their clothes were simple and didn't change much over the centuries. They did wear plenty of showy ornaments, though. Richer people wore fancier clothers and a wider range of accessories, too.

DAY-TO-DAY WEAR

Most clothes were made of linen. Rich people wore very thin, fine linen, while ordinary people wore a thicker, coarser cloth. Until the New Kingdom, women wore a simple, tight-fitting ankle-length dress, with two shoulder straps. Men wore a kilt, made from a piece of linen wrapped around the waist and tucked in. This could be either knee or ankle length. In winter, men and women sometimes wore cloaks made from thick linen.

A servant girl wearing a brightly patterned dress

Egyptians went barefoot most of the time. They sometimes wore sandals made of papyrus reeds, and nobles had sandals made of richly decorated leather.

A CHANGE OF STYLE

During the New Kingdom, tunics and cloaks made of very fine pleated linen became fashionable for both men and women. The pleats would have made the fabric hang very elegantly. Women began to wear another garment over their basic tunic, which as well as having pleats sometimes had a bright fringe with little ornaments attached to it. Some men had two kilts – a longer one made of the finest, almost transparent linen, was worn over the basic short tunic.

These statues are of an Old Kingdom couple, Rahotep and Nofret. Rahotep wears a simple kilt and Nofret a dress, wig and cloak.

This New Kingdom tomb painting shows the more elaborate fashions for men and women, which used much more fabric, with many pleats.

Chunky bracelets like this were worn on the upper arm

These necklaces are made of gold and semi-precious stones.

FINE ORNAMENTS

No Egyptian's costume was complete without a selection of amulets, necklaces, bracelets and other ornaments. Poor people's were made from cheaper substances such as copper or faience. The rich wore spectacular pieces made from gold, silver and electrum, often set with semi-precious stones and glass.

The most striking items were the big decorative collars that were often worn by servants as well as their masters. These were usually made of several strings of beads or jewels that sat in a big semi-circle around the neck. Women wore them more often than men, but they were popular among both sexes.

WIGS AND HAIRCUTS

Most men kept their hair very short, though noblemen often had longer hair. They were generally clean-shaven (Rahotep's moustache is unusual – see left). Boys shaved their heads, apart from one section that formed a kind of pony-tail to one side. This was called the 'side-lock of youth'. Women wore their long hair either loose or braided in a variety of styles, and decorated it with flowers, pins and beads.

At parties, both men and women wore wigs. Among the rich these could be amazingly elaborate, especially in later periods, with lots of braids and curls. The wigs also had ornaments hung over them, or were decorated with beads and jewels. The best wigs were made of real hair, but there were cheaper ones of black wool.

This young boy has a 'side-lock of youth', the usual hairstyle for boys of his age, and plenty of ornaments.

The painting on the right is of a New Kingdom woman wearing a long, elaborate wig, decorated with a sacred blue lotus flower.

⬥ INTERNET LINK

At **www.usborne-quicklinks.com** you'll find a link to the **Seattle Art Museum Web site**, where you can help the Egyptian barber create new hairstyles for his customers.

The cone on top of her head is made of perfumed fat.

TRAVEL AND TRANSPORT

The river Nile was like a big main road that stretched from one end of the country to the other. Real roads would have been a waste of precious farming land in the Nile valley, and in any case the annual flood would have washed them away. So most travel in ancient Egypt happened in boats.

SHORT TRIPS

Ordinary people didn't travel very much. They only needed to cross the river, and go short distances up and down. From the earliest times, they made small boats out of bundles of reeds, and went on using these for getting around and fishing throughout ancient Egyptian history. From the Old Kingdom onwards, though, all boats of any size (such as passenger ferries) were made of wood.

UP AND DOWNRIVER

Sailing north by river was easy, because this is the way the Nile flows. Luckily, though, the wind usually blows from the north. This means that with a sail you can travel south, against the flow of the river. So, when you see carvings or paintings of Egyptian ships, you can tell which way they're going by whether their sail is up or not.

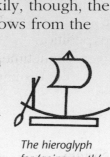

The hieroglyph for 'going south' showed a ship with its sail up.

The hieroglyph for 'going north' showed the sail rolled down.

THE BUSY RIVER

People used the Nile a great deal for getting around, but it was also the place where they relaxed and had fun. For nobles in particular, being on the river in a nice boat was a pleasant way to pass some time. These boats often had a cabin with a canopy in front, to shield their passengers from the sun.

Hunting birds, crocodiles and hippopotamuses were all popular pastimes, and people loved playing around in the water. Groups of boatmen often held competitions, where two teams on boats would try to knock each other into the river.

A nobleman's boat with a canopy to protect him from the sun

A small local passenger ferry

CARRYING CARGOES

The Egyptians depended on the Nile to help them transport goods, and they needed particularly big, strong boats to carry heavy loads. Some of the heaviest loads of all were the blocks of stone used in building projects. For the larger ones, huge barges were used. These barges were too big to be rowed, so they were towed by as many as 27 smaller boats.

One of the biggest barges on record was used to transport Hatshepsut's granite obelisks from Aswan to the temples at Karnak. It was estimated to be 82m (260ft) long.

The Nile was always busy, with many different kinds of boats making their way up and down.

THE OPEN SEA

Egypt's traders sailed from the Mediterranean coast to other eastern Mediterranean countries, and crossed the eastern desert to the Red Sea to reach places such as Punt. Sea-going ships for trading expeditions to the Red Sea were sometimes built along the Nile, dismantled and carried to the sea, where they were reassembled. They were strong, and had plenty of storage space. You can see what they looked like on page 24.

A huge barge carrying an obelisk up the river. These barges were too big to row, so they were towed by lots of little boats.

TRAVEL ON LAND

Although the Egyptians used the Nile whenever possible, overland travel was sometimes unavoidable. Generally, this had to be on foot, though on journeys across the desert, people and small loads were carried by donkey.

For the rich, overland travel was a bit more comfortable. Nobles sometimes travelled in special carrying chairs carried by slaves, or in litters, which were slung between donkeys. Some of them also owned horse-drawn chariots.

INTERNET LINK

*At **www.usborne-quicklinks.com** you'll find a link to a Web site where you can read more about Egyptian boats, including information on some exciting new discoveries.*

Fishermen used small wooden boats like these.

Boatmen playing the popular game of pushing each other off their reed boats

Reed boat

This nobleman is being carried in his chair by Nubian servants.

MEDICINE AND MAGIC

Egyptian doctors were highly respected throughout the Middle East. Sometimes, they were even summoned abroad to treat foreign princes. Egyptian medicine was closely linked to religion, so when science didn't work, doctors turned to magic instead.

This papyrus, now known as the 'London Medical Papyrus', gives recipes and spells for curing different illnesses.

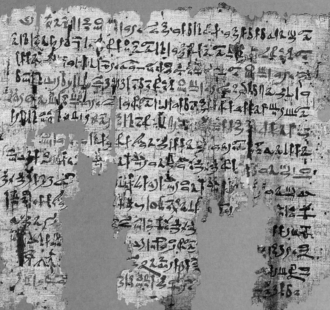

WHO WERE DOCTORS?

Doctors may have passed their knowledge from father to son, although there were probably medical schools as well. Once they had finished their training and were officially recognized as doctors, they received a salary from the government.

Most doctors worked as general practitioners in the community. Others worked in temples, or as army surgeons or specialist consultants. The most skilled doctors were appointed physicians to the royal court.

WHAT THEY KNEW

Egyptian doctors understood quite a lot about the body. They knew that the heart pumps blood around, and they had some understanding of the nervous system. They were also skilled at setting bones. But there were big gaps in their knowledge. They thought that water, air and nerves passed through the heart. They also believed that people thought with their hearts and that the brain was useless.

A bone showing clearly where it broke and healed again. There were no plaster casts, so bones often didn't heal quite straight.

TRIAL AND ERROR

Egyptian doctors learned about drugs and treatments through trial and error. They knew that a good diet was important, and believed that too much food caused diseases and polluted the body. They understood that rest and hygiene could prevent illnesses, and could also help cure them.

 INTERNET LINK

At **www.usborne-quicklinks.com** you'll find a link to a Web site which has a detailed article about ancient Egyptian doctors, describing how much they knew about the human body.

BOOKS AND POTIONS

Doctors had textbooks they could consult on how to diagnose and treat illnesses. There were also books on anatomy, women's diseases, dentistry, surgery and veterinary science.

When treating someone, doctors followed a strict procedure. They looked for the symptoms, then asked questions, inspected, felt, smelled and probed. They took detailed notes, and recorded the treatment and the results. These notes were then used in future cases.

The castor oil plant, shown here, was often used in Egyptian remedies. Many of the other ingredients are unknown, because we still can't read their particular hieroglyphs.

Honey and garlic, like castor oil, appear in many Egyptian remedies. Honey was also used for keeping wounds clean.

Medicines were made from different plants, minerals and sometimes parts of animals. These were either mixed with water, beer, wine or milk and drunk, or mixed with oil and applied to the skin.

THE ROLE OF RELIGION

To the Egyptians, any illness was caused by evil spirits entering the body, so special prayers to the gods were recited over the patient during treatment. If all their efforts with medicines failed, doctors turned to religion and magic for a solution. For this reason, Egyptian doctors consisted of three groups: surgeon-healers, priest-doctors, and pure magicians.

An opium bottle. Opium was an early anaesthetic, used to deaden pain.

GODS AND MAGICIANS

The gods Thoth, Sekhmet, Isis and Imhotep were particularly associated with healing, and people often went to their temples to find a cure. Sometimes, they were allowed to spend the night in a room next to the temple, so that the gods could visit them in dreams – another source of information about how to treat someone. If everything failed, a magician could be called in. He recited spells or used ivory wands to draw magic circles of protection around the sick person.

This ivory magic wand was meant to give protection during childbirth.

BEAUTY CARE

The Egyptians kept themselves very clean, and paid a lot of attention to the finer details of their looks. Both men and women wore perfume and cosmetics which they kept in elegant little pots.

FINISHING TOUCHES

Many cosmetics were made from finely ground minerals mixed with oils. Egyptians were particularly fond of eyeliner. Malachite (copper ore) was used to make green or grey eyepaint called kohl. This emphasized the beauty of someone's eyes, and also cut down the glare of the sun. Lipstick and blusher were popular as well. These were made with red ochre, a type of clay.

Red-brown henna, made from the leaves of the henna tree, was used to paint nails, and possibly hands and feet as well.

This glass container was probably used to hold perfume.

SMELLING SWEET

It was important to keep clean in the hot climate. Most people washed in the river, or used a basin and jug of water at home. Instead of soap, they used a cleansing cream made from oil, lime and perfume. They also rubbed scented oils into their skin to stop it from drying out in the fierce sun.

Perfumes were made from flowers, seeds and fruits soaked in oils and animal fats. In wall paintings, perfume is often shown as little cones that people wore on their heads at parties (see page 89).

Lotus blossoms were used to make perfume, and were also worn in women's hair.

Images on coffins, like the one above, suggest how women wore eye makeup.

Mirrors, like this bronze one, were just highly polished metal.

Rich people kept their toiletries in elaborate boxes like the one below.

INTERNET LINK

At **www.usborne-quicklinks.com** you'll find a link to a Web site where you can watch a short movie about Egyptian cosmetics, and the beautiful containers they made for them.

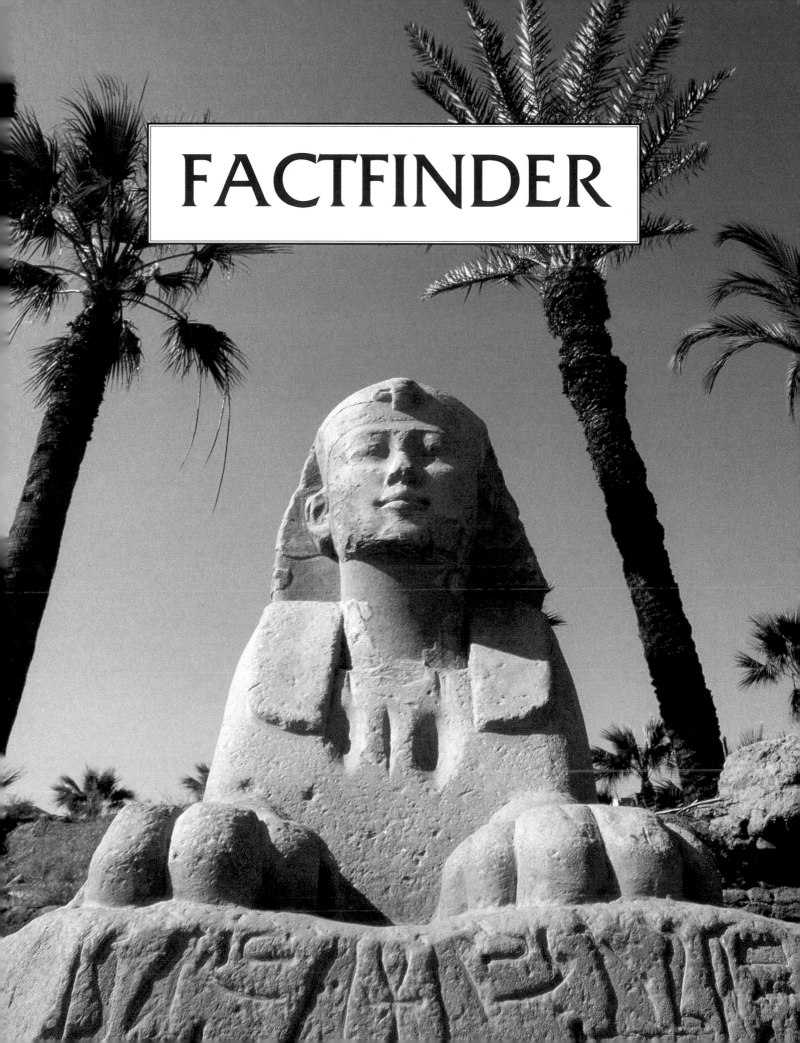

FACTFINDER

TIME CHART

This time chart outlines the major events in the history of Ancient Egypt. It also shows - with square bullet points - important things that were happening in other parts of the world at the same time. Some of the dates have a letter "c." in front of them. This means that experts aren't sure precisely when the event happened. The "c." stands for *circa*, which means "about" in Latin.

c.5500BC People start to settle on the banks of the Nile in Egypt.

■ **c.5000BC** Gradual introduction of farming in China and central America.

■ **c.4000BC** Uruk culture develops in Sumer in Mesopotamia.

■ **c.4000BC** Farming communities settle in the Indus Valley, India.

■ **c.3500BC** Writing develops in Sumer. The Sumerians also invent the wheel and learn how to make bronze.

THE PREDYNASTIC PERIOD
c.3500-3100BC

People start to farm the land, and dig irrigation canals. Gradually two separate kingdoms emerge: Upper Egypt in the south and Lower Egypt in the North.

c.3300-3100BC Hieroglyphic (picture) writing develops in Egypt.

Some hieroglyphs copied from the walls of a temple

c.3100BC Upper and Lower Egypt are united by King Menes.

THE ARCHAIC PERIOD
c.3100-2649BC

■ **c.3000-2000BC** Independent city states flourish in Sumer, Akkad and Canaan. Early Bronze Age in Canaan.

■ **c.3000-1100BC** Bronze Age in Greece.

■ **c.3000BC** Pottery in use in Ecuador.

■ **c.2900-2400BC** Early dynasties develop in Sumer.

THE OLD KINGDOM
c.2649-2150BC

This is the period of pyramid building in Egypt.

c.2590BC The Great Pyramid of Giza, the pyramid of Khufu (or Cheops), is built.

■ **c.2500BC** Longshan culture in China.

■ **c.2500-1800BC** Indus Valley Civilization in India. The people have huge cities with large buildings, good sanitation and a form of writing.

■ **c.2500-1500BC** Stonehenge is built in Britain.

■ **c.2371BC** Sargon of Akkad seizes the throne of the city of Kish and builds up an empire in Mesopotamia.

■ **c.2350-2150** Kingdom of Akkad is established in Mesopotamia.

■ **c.2205-1766BC** Traditional dates for legendary Xia Dynasty in China.

c.2150-2040BC First Intermediate Period in Egypt.

■ **c.2100-2000BC** Dynasty III of Ur rules over Sumer and Akkad.

THE MIDDLE KINGDOM
c.2040-1640BC

■ **c.2000BC** Amorites conquer Mesopotamia and Assyria and set up independent city states in Canaan. Indo-Europeans spread into the Middle East.

■ **By c.2000BC** Flourishing civilization on Crete.

This young man comes from a wall-painting in the palace of Knossos in Crete.

■ **c.2000-1500** Middle Bronze Age in Canaan.

■ **c.2000-1450** The Old Assyrian Empire.

■ **c.2000-1000BC** Hurrians form an aristocratic caste in cities in Canaan ruling the Amorites and Canaanites.

■ **c.2000-1000BC** Beginning of Mayan culture in central America.

■ **c.2000BC** Evidence of farming, metal-working and pottery in Peru.

■ **c.2000BC** Horses and wheeled vehicles are being used in eastern Europe.

■ **c.1900BC** Palaces are built on Crete.

■ **c.1813-1781BC** Reign of Shamshi-Adad of Assyria. He builds up an empire from Mari to Babylon.

■ **c.1792-1750BC** Reign of Hammurabi of Babylon.

■ **c.1766-1027BC** Shang Dynasty in China. A feudal state with walled cities and temples, ruled by priest-kings.

■ **c.1740BC** Hittites are united as one kingdom.

■ **c.1700BC** Cretan palaces are destroyed by earthquakes and then rebuilt.

Reconstruction of the walled city of Mycenae in Greece

c.1674-1720BC Nile Delta is overrun by Hyksos from the Middle East.

c.1640-1552BC Second Intermediate Period. Egypt rules Kush (Sudan).

■ **c.1600BC** Rise of the Mycenaean culture in Greece.

THE NEW KINGDOM
c.1552-1069BC

The greatest period of the Egyptian empire. Royal tombs are built in the Valley of the Kings.

■ **c.1500BC** Indo-Europeans known as Aryans arrive in India.

■ **c.1500BC** Mitannians unite and rule Hurrian kingdoms.

■ **c.1595BC** Hittites plunder Babylon and destroy the Amorite kingdom.

■ **c.1570-1158BC** Kassite dynasty rules in Babylon.

■ **c.1550-1150BC** Late Bronze Age in Canaan.

■ **c.1500BC** Aryans settle in Persia, now called Iran.

■ **c.1500BC** Writing develops in China.

■ **c.1500BC** Farming reaches the southeast of North America.

■ **c.1500BC** Decline of the Indus Valley civilization in India.

■ **c.1500-600BC** Vedic Period in India: Hindu religion gradually established.

■ **c.1500BC-AD200** Rise of the Olmec culture in Mexico: they use picture writing and calendars, and build huge temples and stone heads.

1490-1468BC Reign of Hatshepsut, woman pharaoh of Egypt.

1490-1436BC Reign of Tuthmosis III in Egypt: greatest of the warrior pharaohs.

■ **c.1450BC** Volcanic eruption on Thera. Minoan civilization comes to an end. Palaces are destroyed and Crete is taken over by Mycenaeans.

■ **c.1450-1390BC** Mitanni conquer Assyria and build an empire from the Zagros mountains to the Mediterranean Sea.

■ **c.1450-1200BC** Hittite New Kingdom.

■ **1440BC** Mitanni make peace treaty with Egypt.

■ **1380BC** Accession of Shuppiluliuma, one of the greatest Hittite kings. He overthrows the Mitanni and captures Syria, part of the Egyptian empire.

1364-1347BC Reign of Akhenaten (Amenhotep IV), the king who led a religious revolution in Egypt.

Nefertiti, wife of Akhenaten

■ **c.1363-1000BC** The Middle Assyrian Empire

1347-1337BC Reign of Tutankhamun.

■ **c.1300BC** Bronze Age culture in Europe known as Urnfield.

1289-1224BC Reign of Ramesses II; a great warrior and builder.

1284BC Battle of Kadesh: Ramesses II fights the Hittites.

■ **c.1250BC** Trojan Wars between Troy (in Turkey) and Mycenaeans: Troy is destroyed.

■ **c.1250BC** Hebrews first arrive in Canaan.

■ **c.1200-300BC** Chavín people create the first civilization in South America: they build huge temples and make things with gold.

■ **c.1200BC** Decline of Mycenaean culture in Greece.

■ **c.1200BC** The advance of the Sea Peoples, raiders and settlers from Greece and Mediterranean islands.

A sea battle between the Sea Peoples and the Egyptians, based on a carving at Luxor

1200-1194BC Reign of Seti II.

■ **1196-1195BC** Sea Peoples destroy the Hittite empire. Some Hittites establish small Neo-Hittite states.

1184-1153BC Reign of Ramesses III; the last great warrior pharaoh. He defeats the Sea Peoples.

c.1150BC Peleset, or Philistines, a group of Sea Peoples, settle in Canaan, later known as Palestine after them.

■ **c.1158BC** Kassite rulers are thrown out of Babylon. After an unsettled period Babylonian rule is restored.

■ **c.1100BC** Phoenicians are established in Canaan. They found colonies on the southern and western shores of the Mediterranean, with cities at Byblos, Sidon, Beirut and Tyre.

c.1085BC Nubia and Kush regain independence from Egypt.

1069-664BC The Third Intermediate Period in Egypt.

■ **1027-221BC** Zhou dynasty overthrows the Shang in China. A period of trade and growth, but also of instability and wars.

■ **c.1020-1010BC** Reign of Saul, first King of the Israelites.

■ **c.1000-612BC** The New Assyrian Empire; the greatest period of conquest and expansion.

■ **c.1000-300BC** Adena people begin building earth mounds in North America.

■ **c.1000BC** The Latins first settle on the Palatine Hill in Rome.

■ **c.970-930BC** Reign of King Solomon of the Israelites. Israelite power reaches its height.

■ **c.911BC** New Assyrian Empire begins.

■ **c.900BC** The *Rig Veda* is composed in India.

■ **c.814BC** Phoenicians found the city of Carthage in North Africa.

■ **c.800BC** Hindu religion spreads south in India.

Shiva the destroyer, one of the many Hindu gods

■ **c.800BC** Celtic way of life spreads across western Europe.

■ **c.800-500BC** Archaic Period in Greece: an alphabet is introduced, first Olympic Games are held and Homer composes the *Iliad* and *Odyssey* (tales of the Trojan Wars).

■ **c.800-400BC** Etruscans flourish in central and northern Italy.

■ **c.753BC** Traditional date for the founding of Rome.

728BC Egypt is conquered by Piankhi, a Nubian king.

■ **726-722BC** Reign of Shalmaneser V of Assyria who conquers the kingdom of Israel.

■ **c.722-481BC** Spring and Autumn Period in China; small states fight for supremacy.

■ **721-705BC** Reign of Sargon II of Assyria.

■ **c.700BC** Achaemenid dynasty in Persia.

■ **c.670BC** Kingdom of Medea set up near Persia.

**THE LATE PERIOD
664-525BC**

664-525BC Saite dynasty rules Egypt: Egyptian independence is restored.

■ **668-627BC** Reign of Ashurbanipal II of Assyria; he sacks Thebes (in Egypt), Babylon and Susa (Persia).

■ **c.650BC** The first coins are introduced in Lydia.

■ **626-539BC** The New Babylonian empire.

■ **612BC** Ashur and Nineveh fall to the Medes and Babylonians.

■ **605-562BC** Reign of Nebuchadnezzar II of Babylon.

c.600-500BC Nubians abandon their capital at Napata and move south to Meroë.

■ **c.600BC** Introduction of Taoism in China by the prophet Lao-zi.

■ **597BC** Nebuchadnezzar II of Babylon occupies Jerusalem and carries off many of its leading citizens to Babylon. After a further revolt in **587-568BC** he sacks Jerusalem and again deports many of the people to Babylon.

■ **c.560-483BC** The life of Gautama Siddhartha, the Buddha.

■ **551-479BC** Life of Kong zi (also known as Confucius), Chinese philosopher and prophet.

The Chinese prophet and philosopher Confucius

■ **c.550BC** Medea and Persia are united by Cyrus II of Persia. He conquers Lydia and takes over the Babylonian empire.

THE PERSIAN PERIOD
525-331BC

525BC Egypt is conquered by Cambyses II of Persia.

Persian elite warrior, known as an 'Immortal', taken from the palace at Susa

■ **c.510BC** Rome becomes a republic.

■ **c.500-336BC** Classical Period in Greece: the great age of Greek civilization.

■ **490-449BC** Wars between Greece and Persia.

■ **c.481-221BC** Warring States Period in China; seven major states destroy each other in struggles for power.

■ **c.465BC** Persia declines.

■ **447-438BC** The Parthenon temple is built in Athens.

404-343BC Egyptians overthrow the Persians.

343-331BC The Persians retake Egypt.

THE GREEK PERIOD
332-323BC

332BC Alexander the Great of Macedonia conquers the Persian empire. He is accepted by the Egyptians as pharaoh.

323BC Alexandria becomes the new capital of Egypt. Alexander the Great dies.

323BC Egypt comes under the control of General Ptolemy.

323-281BC Wars of the Diadochi (Alexander's generals).

301-64BC Ptolemaic dynasty rules Egypt.

■ **c.300BC** Mayan people begin building stone cities in central America.

c.300-200BC Alphabetic script is developed in Meroë.

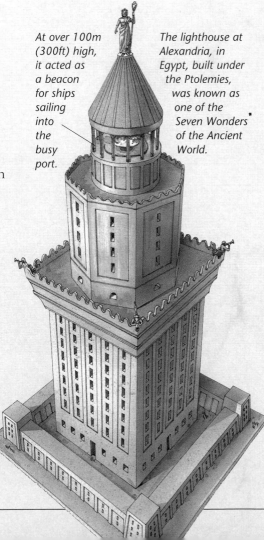

At over 100m (300ft) high, it acted as a beacon for ships sailing into the busy port.

The lighthouse at Alexandria, in Egypt, built under the Ptolemies, was known as one of the Seven Wonders of the Ancient World.

■ **280-268BC** The Antigonid dynasty rules in Macedonia.

■ **c.272-231BC** Asoka of the Maurya dynasty unites most of India under his rule.

■ **264BC** Rome now dominates all Italy.

■ **264-241BC** First Punic War between Rome and Carthage.

■ **221BC** Unification of China under the first Ch'in emperor Shi-huang-ti.

■ **218 202BC** Second Punic War.

■ **214BC** Great Wall of China is built to keep out hostile tribes of the Hsiung-Nu (or Huns).

■ **206BC-AD222** Han dynasty rules China.

■ **c.200BC** Nazca people make giant drawings in the deserts of Peru.

■ **149-146BC** Third Punic War: Carthage is destroyed.

■ **133-31BC** The Romans expand throughout the Mediterranean.

■ **c.100BC** Paper is invented in China.

■ **c.100BC** People in central America start building the vast pyramid city of Teotihuacan.

■ **58-51BC** Julius Caesar, a Roman political leader and general, conquers Gaul (France).

■ **55-54BC** Caesar invades Britain.

Coin showing Caesar's head

51-30BC Reign of Cleopatra VII of Egypt.

31BC Cleopatra and her Roman lover Mark Antony are defeated by Roman forces led by Octavian (later Emperor Augustus) at the Battle of Actium, off the western coast of Greece. They both commit suicide, rather than surrender.

30BC Egypt becomes a province of the Roman empire.

KINGS & DYNASTIES

Here are the names and approximate dates of most of the kings - and some queens - and dynasties that ruled Egypt right up to the Roman conquest in 30BC.

The reign dates can be confusing, because sometimes - especially during the Intermediate periods - several kings ruled different parts of Egypt at the same time. Some kings have two names, as they are sometimes known by the names the Greeks gave them (shown in brackets). Names marked * show kings crowned in the lifetime of the previous king. Those marked ** are queens ruling as kings.

The evidence for Egyptian dates comes from lists of kings compiled by the Egyptians themselves. Some dates may vary a little in other books. This is because experts disagree about how to interpret the available evidence, and often use slightly different dating systems.

Wall-painting of geese from an Old Kingdom tomb at Meidum

THE ARCHAIC PERIOD
(c.3100-2649BC)

Very few dates are known from this early period in Egyptian history.

Dynasty I
Seven or eight kings starting with:

Menes c.3100, Narmer, Hor-Aha

Carving showing the King of Upper Egypt defeating the ruler of Lower Egypt

Dynasty II
Eight or nine kings including:

Hetepsekhemwy, Re'neb, Peribsen and **Kha'sekhemui**

THE OLD KINGDOM
(c.2649-2150BC)

Dynasty III

Sanakht	c.2649-2630BC
Djoser	c.2630-2611BC
Sekhemkhet	c.2611-2603BC
Kha'ba	c.2603-2599BC
Huni	c.2599-2575BC

Dynasty IV

Seneferu	c.2575-2551BC
Khufu (Cheops)	c.2551-2528BC
Ra'djedef	c.2528-2520BC
Khafre (Khephren)	c.2520-2494BC
Menkaure (Mycerinus)	c.2490-2472BC
Shepseskaf	c.2472-2467BC

Dynasty V

Userkaf	c.2465-2323BC
Sahure	c.2458-2446BC
Neferirkare	c.2446-2426BC
Shepseskare	c.2426-2419BC
Ra'neferef	c.2419-2416BC
Neuserre	c.2416-2392BC
Menkauhor	c.2396-2388BC
Djedkare	c2388-2356BC
Unas	c.2356-2323BC

Dynasty VI

Teti	c.2323-2291BC
Pepi I	c.2289-2255BC
Merenre	c.2255-2246BC
Pepi II	c.2246-2152BC
Nitocris**	c.2152-2150BC

FIRST INTERMEDIATE PERIOD
(c.2150- 2040BC)

Dynasties VII and VIII
(c.2150-2134BC)

These dynasties were made up of numbers of kings who reigned only for short periods.

Dynasties IX and X
(c.2134-2040BC)

These kings ruled from the city of Herakleopolis.

Statue of Pepi II with his mother, Meryre-ankhnes

THE MIDDLE KINGDOM
(c.2040-1640BC)

A line of kings reigned independently at Thebes, at the same time as the kings of Herakleopolis. This family later became Dynasty XI, ruling over Egypt under the Middle Kingdom.

Dynasty XI

Mentuhotep II	c.2040-2010BC
Mentuhotep III	c.2010-1998BC
Mentuhotep III	c.1998-1991BC

Dynasty XII

Amenemhat I	c.1991-1962 BC
Senusret I*	c.1971-1926BC
Amenemhat II*	c.1929-1892BC
Senusret II*	c.1897-1878BC
Senusret III*	c.1878-1841BC
Amenemhat III*	c.1844-1797BC
Amenemhat IV*	c.1799-1787BC
Sobek-neferu**	c.1787-1783BC

Dynasty XIII
(c.1783-1640BC)

Dynasty XIII was made up of about 70 kings, most of whom had very short reigns.

Dynasty XIV

Dynasty XIV is the name given to princes from the western delta who broke away, ruling at the same time as Dynasty XIII.

The pharaoh's blue crown, known as a khepresh

SECOND INTERMEDIATE PERIOD
(c.1640-1552BC)

Dynasty XV

This dynasty was made up of Hyksos kings including:
Apophis (c.1585-1542BC).

Dynasty XVI

Minor kings who ruled at the same time as Dynasty XV.

Dynasty XVII
(c.1640-1552BC)

This dynasty contained fifteen Theban kings including:
Tao I, Tao II and **Kamose (c.1555-1552BC)**

THE NEW KINGDOM
(1552-1069BC)

Dynasty XVIII

Ahmose	c.1552-1527BC
Amenhotep I	c.1527-1506BC
Tuthmosis I	c.1506-1494BC
Tuthmosis II	c.1494-1490BC
Hatshepsut**	c.1490-1468BC
Tuthmosis III	c.1490-1436BC
Amenhotep II	c.1438-1412BC
Tuthmosis IV	c.1412-1402BC
Amenhotep III	c.1402-1364BC
Akhenaten (Amenhotep IV)	c.1364-1347BC
Smenkhkare*	c.1351-1348BC
Tutankhamun	c.1347-1337BC
Ay	c.1337-1333BC
Horemheb	c.1333-1305BC

Statue of Queen Hatshepsut, shown with a beard

Horemheb

Dynasty XIX

Ramesses I	c.1305-1303BC
Seti I	c.1303-1289BC
Ramesses II	c.1289-1224BC
Merenptah	c.1224-1204BC
Amenmesse	c.1204-1200BC
Seti II	c.1200-1194BC
Siptah	c.1194-1188BC
Tawosret**	c.1194-1186BC

Dynasty XX

Set-nakht	c.1186-1184BC
Ramesses III	c.1184-1153BC
Ramesses IV	c.1153-1146BC
Ramesses V	c.1146-1142BC
Ramesses VI	c.1142-1135BC
Ramesses VII	c.1135-1129BC
Ramesses VIII	c.1129-1127BC
Ramesses IX	c.1127-1109BC
Ramesses X	c.1109-1099BC
Ramesses XI	c.1099-1069BC

By the end of Dynasty XX, Egypt was divided and a line of priests, beginning with Heri-Hor, was ruling from Thebes.

THIRD INTERMEDIATE PERIOD
(1069-664BC)

Dynasty XXI
This line of kings ruled part of the country from Tanis.

Smendes I	c.1069-1043BC
Amenemnisu	c.1043-1039BC
Psusennes I	c.1039-991BC
Amenemope	c.993-984BC
Osochor	c.984-978BC
Si-Amun	c.978-959BC
Psusennes II	c.959-945BC

Dynasty XXII
This line of Libyan kings began reuniting the country.

Shoshenq I	c.945-924BC
Osorkon I 9	c.24-889BC
Shoshenq II	c.890BC
Takeloth I	c.89-874BC
Osorkon II	c.874-850BC
Takeloth II	c.850-825BC
Shoshenq III	c.825-773BC
Pimay	c.773-767BC
Shoshenq V	c.767-730BC
Osorkon IV	c.730-715BC

Dynasty XXIII & Dynasty XXIV
These were two separate lines of kings ruling at the same time as the later kings of Dynasty XXII. They included:

Tefnakhte I	c.727-720BC
Bakenranef	c.720-715BC

Dynasty XXV
THE NUBIAN KINGS

Piankhi	c.728-716BC
Shabako	c.716-702BC
Shebitku	c.702-690BC
Taharqa	c.690-664BC
Tanut-Amun	c.664-663BC

THE LATE PERIOD
(664-525BC)

Dynasty XXVI
THE SAITE KINGS

Psamtek I	c.664-610BC
Necho II	c.610-595BC
Psamtek II	c.595-589BC
Apries	c.589-570BC
Amasis	c.570-526BC
Psamtek III	c.526-525BC

Cleopatra VII

THE PERSIAN PERIOD
(525-332BC)

Dynasty XXVII (525-404BC)
A line of Persian kings including: **Cambyses (525-521BC) Darius I (521-485BC)** and **Xerxes (485-464BC)**

Dynasty XXVIII

Amyrtaeus	c.404-399BC

Dynasty XXIX

Nepherites I	c.399-393BC
Achoris	c.393-380BC
Psammuthis	c.380-379BC
Nepherites II	c.379BC

Dynasty XXX

Nectanebo I	c.379-361BC
Tachos	c.361-359BC
Nectanebo II	c.359-342BC

Dynasty XXXI (341-323BC) A second line of Persian kings.

THE MACEDONIAN KINGS
(332-305BC)

Alexander the Great	332-323BC
Philip Arrhidaeus	323-316BC
Alexander IV	316-305BC

THE PTOLEMIES
(305-30BC)

Ptolemy I	305-284BC
Ptolemy II	284-246BC
Ptolemy III	246-221BC
Ptolemy IV	221-205BC
Ptolemy V	205-180BC
Ptolemy VI	160-164BC and 163-145BC
Ptolemy VII	145BC
Ptolemy VIII	170-163BC and 145-116BC
Queen Cleopatra III and **Ptolemy IX**	116-107BC
Queen Cleopatra III and **Ptolemy X**	107-88BC
Ptolemy IX	88-81BC
Queen Cleopatra Berenice	81-80BC
Ptolemy XI	80BC
Ptolemy XII	80-58BC
Queen Berenice IV	58-55BC
Ptolemy XII	55-51BC
Queen Cleopatra VII	51-30BC
with **Ptolemy XIII**	(51-47BC)
with **Ptolemy XIV**	(47-44BC)
and with **Ptolemy XV**	(44-30BC)

WHO'S WHO

The next five pages give you a brief outline of some of the most important and influential people in Egypt and other civilizations around the Middle East in ancient times. Names that appear in **bold type** also have their own entries. Dates of reigns, where known, are shown in brackets.

AHHOTEP I
Queen of Egypt (Dynasty XVII). Daughter of Tao I and Teti-sheri, and sister-wife of **Tao II**. She acted as regent during the reign of her son **Ahmose**.

AHMES NEFERTARI
Queen of Egypt (Dynasty XVIII). Daughter of **Tao II** and **Ahhotep I**, and sister wife of **Ahmose**. She held the offices of God's Wife and of Second Prophet of Amun in the temple at Karnak and acted as regent for her fourth son, Amenhotep I. Together they founded the community of royal tomb-builders, who eventually settled in the village of Deir el Medina (see page 74).

AHMOSE (c.1552-1527BC)
King of Egypt. The first king of Dynasty XVIII and the New Kingdom. Son of **Tao II** and **Ahhtotep I**, he came to the throne as a child, with his mother as regent. Ahmose continued the war begun by his father and brother and succeeded in liberating Egypt from the Hyksos. After suppressing rebellions at home, he began the reconquest of Nubia.

AHMOSE OF EL KAB
(Dynasty XVII/XVIII). Egyptian soldier in the army of King **Ahmose**. He fought on campaigns to drive the Hyksos from Egypt and won the 'Gold of Valour', the highest award for bravery. The biography on the walls of his tomb is an important source of information about the Egyptian wars against the Hyksos.

AKHENATEN/AMENHOTEP IV (c.1364-1347BC)
King of Egypt (Dynasty XVIII). One of the most controversial figures in ancient history. He abandoned the traditional Egyptian deities and introduced the worship of one god, the disc of the sun, know as Aten. He changed his name to Akhenaten and built a new capital, Akhetaten. After his death, all these changes were reversed and the capital was abandoned. Akhenaten's monuments were destroyed and he himself was branded as a heretic.

ALEXANDER THE GREAT (332-323BC)
King of Macedonia, military leader and empire builder. After taking control of Greece, he marched into Asia Minor and conquered the entire Persian empire (including Egypt). He founded many new cities, the most famous of which was the port of Alexandria in Egypt, which became the new capital. Alexander married a Persian princess called Roxane and died in Babylon at the age of 32. His heirs were eventually murdered and the empire was divided up between his generals. One of these, **Ptolemy**, became King of Egypt and founded the Ptolemaic Dynasty.

Alexander the Great

AMENEMHAT I (c.1991-1962BC)
First king of Dynasty XII. To secure the succession, he had his son Senusret I crowned during his lifetime. Amenemhat was murdered, but Senusret remained in control.

AMENHOTEP III (c.1402-1364BC)
King of Egypt (Dynasty XVIII) in a period of peace and stability. Son of Tuthmosis IV. He built the Colossi of Memnon. Towards the end of his reign, the revolutionary artistic styles of Amarna began to appear, which suggests he may have taken his son **Akhenaten** as co-ruler. Akhenaten's religious ideas may also have begun to develop in his father's reign.

AMENHOTEP IV, see **Akhenaten**.

AMENHOTEP, SON OF HAPU
Egyptian royal scribe during the reign of Amenhotep III. He held some of the highest offices in the land and his statues were erected in the temples of Amun and Mut at Karnak. He was worshipped as a god in the Late Period in Thebes.

AMENIRDIS II
Nubian princess and God's Wife. Daughter of King **Taharqa** (Dynasty XXV). She was obliged to adopt **Nitocris**, the daughter of Psamtek I, first king of Dynasty XXVI, as heir.

ANKHESENPAAMUN
Queen of Egypt (Dynasty XVIII). Sister-wife of **Tutankhamun**. After he died she wrote to **Shuppiliuma**, King of the Hittites, offering to marry one of his sons and make him King of Egypt. But the plot was discovered and the Hittite prince was murdered. She married Ay, an elderly courtier who became king.

ANTONY, MARK
Roman soldier and politician. Lover of **Cleopatra VII**, he ruled Egypt with her after the death of **Caesar**. War broke out after a quarrel with Caesar's heir Octavian. Anthony and Cleopatra were defeated at the Battle of Actium and committed suicide.

APOPHIS (c.1585-1542BC)

One of the greatest of the Hyksos kings of Egypt (Dynasty XV). During his reign, war broke out with **Tao II**, the King of Thebes. This led to the expulsion of the Hyksos and the start of the New Kingdom.

BAY

An adventurer of Syrian origin who became influential in Egypt at the end of Dynasty XIX. He tried to seize the throne after the death of Queen **Tawosret**.

BINT-ANATH

Queen of Egypt (Dynasty XIX). Daughter and wife of **Ramesses II**. She has a tomb in the Valley of the Queens on the West Bank at Thebes.

CAESAR, JULIUS

Roman politician, writer and general who was made dictator for life. He intervened in a quarrel between his lover **Cleopatra VII** and her brother, and secured the Egyptian throne for her. Murdered on 15 March 44BC.

CAMBYSES (C.525-521BC)

King of Persia. Son of **Cyrus II**. He conquered Egypt in 525BC. He appears to have been a cruel man, and the Greek historian **Herodotus** claimed that he was mad. According to one story, he broke into the a pharaoh's tomb and burned the corpse. He is said to have offended the Egyptians by desecrating temples and wounding the Apis bull.

CLEOPATRA VII (51-30BC)

Queen of Egypt (Ptolemaic Period). Sister-wife of both Ptolemy XIII and Ptolemy XIV and lover of **Julius Caesar**. She later married his friend **Mark Antony**. She and Antony were defeated at the Battle of Actium in 31BC by Caesar's heir Octavian. In 30BC Cleopatra committed suicide and Egypt was absorbed into the Roman empire.

CYRUS II (559-529BC)

King of Persia and founder of the Persian Achaemenid Dynasty. In 550BC, he defeated his grandfather Astyages of Medea and united the kingdoms of Persia and Medea under his rule. He defeated and conquered the kingdom of Lydia and the Babylonian empire.

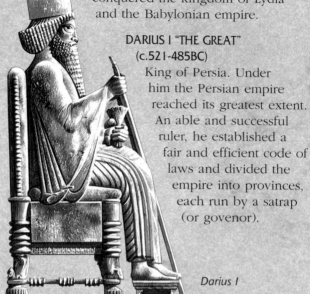

DARIUS I "THE GREAT" (c.521-485BC)

King of Persia. Under him the Persian empire reached its greatest extent. An able and successful ruler, he established a fair and efficient code of laws and divided the empire into provinces, each run by a satrap (or govenor).

Darius I

DJOSER (c.2630-2611BC)

King of Egypt (Dynasty III). The first pyramid, the step pyramid at Saqqara, was designed for him as a tomb by his architect **Imhotep**.

ESARHADDON (680-667BC)

King of Assyria. He rebuilt the city of Babylon, which had been destroyed by his father **Sennacherib**. But he faced great problems. His empire was huge and the Assyrians were cruel and unpopular with their subjects. In 671BC he invaded the Nile Delta and installed Assyrian governors in Egypt.

HATSHEPSUT (1490-1468BC)

Queen of Egypt (Dynasty XVIII). Daughter of Tuthmosis I and Queen **Ahmose** and sister-wife of Tuthmosis II. Appointed regent for his son **Tuthmosis III**, she took power for herself and reigned as 'king' for over 20 years. She has a magnificent mortuary temple at Deir el-Bahri. Evidence of her reign is scarce, as Tuthmosis destroyed her official inscriptions.

HEKANAKHTE

Egyptian priest (Dynasty XI). Letters and documents from his tomb provide an insight into the running of a large estate, and the tensions and intrigues in a wealthy family.

HERI-HOR

Egyptian soldier (Dynasty XX). A member of a family of officials which became influential as the power of the pharaohs declined. During the reign of Ramesses XI, Heri-hor took control of Upper Egypt. Lower Egypt was governed by his son **Smendes**, who married a daughter of Ramesses XI. When Ramesses died, Smendes became the first king of Dynasty XXI.

HERODOTUS (c.450BC)

Greek historian, often known as "the Father of History". He wrote a history of the Greeks based around the Persian Wars. Herodotus was one of the first writers to compare historical facts and to see them as a sequence of linked events.

HETEPHERES I

Queen of Egypt (Dynasty II). Daughter of Huni, sister-wife of **Seneferu** and mother of **Khufu**. Her tomb was robbed and her body destroyed and the remains were moved to Giza. Archaeologists were able to reconstruct the furniture from the surviving gold foil that had covered it.

HOREMHEB (c.1333-1305BC)

King of Egypt (Dynasty XVIII). General and regent in the reign of **Tutankhamun**. He appears to have had no claim to the throne except as husband of Ay's daughter **Mutnodjmet**.

IMHOTEP

Egyptian official (Dynasty III). Architect of the first pyramid, the step pyramid of King **Djoser** at Saqqara. Also a doctor and a high priest, he may have been involved in introducing the calendar. Later generations worshipped him as a god, and the Greeks identified him with their god of medicine, Asclepius.

KAMOSE (c.1555-1552BC)
King of Egypt (Dynasty XVII: the Theban kings). Son of **Tao II** and **Ahhotep I**. He fought with the Hyksos and extended his frontier as far north as the Faiyum. He died in battle and was succeeded by his brother **Ahmose**.

KHAFRE or KHEPHREN (c.2520-2494BC)
King of Egypt (Dynasty IV). Son of **Khufu**, he succeeded his brother Ra'djedef. He and his father were much hated by the Egyptian priests, who told **Herodotus** that "during the reigns of these two pharaohs the Egyptians suffered all kinds of calamities, and for this length of time the temples were closed and never opened". His pyramid is the second one of the three pyramids at Giza, and has the most perfectly preserved temple complex.

KHUFU or CHEOPS (c.2551-2528BC)
King of Egypt (Dynasty IV). Son of **Seneferu** and **Hetepheres I**. His pyramid, the Great Pyramid at Giza, is the largest ever built and was the oldest of the seven wonders of the ancient world. The diorite quarries at Toshka in Nubia were first mined during his reign and a fortified town was built as a trading post at Buhen.

KIYA
One of the secondary wives of **Akhenaten**, possibly the mother of **Tutankhamun**.

MEKET-RE
High-ranking Egyptian official in the reign of Mentuhotep III. His tomb on the West Bank at Thebes contained a magnificent set of tomb models, including models of his villa with its garden and pool, as well as kitchens, workshops, cattle, granaries and boats.

MENES or NARMER (c.3100BC)
Early king of Upper Egypt, conqueror of Lower Egypt and probably first king of a united Egypt under Dynasty I. Menes and Narmer may have been one and the same, but it's also possible they were two separate kings.

MENKAURE or MYCERINUS (c.2490-2472BC)
King of Egypt (Dynasty IV). Son of Khafre. His pyramid is the smallest of the three pyramids at Giza.

MENTUHOTEP II (c.2040-2010BC)
King of Thebes in Upper Egypt (Dynasty XI). In about 2040BC, he defeated the King of Lower Egypt (Dynasty X) and reunited the country under his rule. This began the Middle Kingdom. He built a magnificent mortuary temple and tomb on the west bank of the Nile.

MERENPTAH (c.1224-1204BC)
King of Egypt (Dynasty XIX). He was in his fifties when he succeeded his father **Ramesses II**, who had outlived his first 13 sons. A great military commander, he was involved in battles with the Sea Peoples and the Libyans across Egypt's border. His tomb is in the Valley of the Kings.

MERITATEN
Princess and Queen of Egypt, daughter of **Akhenaten** and **Nefertiti**. She married Smenkhkare, who became pharaoh after Akhenaten's death, but died or was deposed after only a year, and Meritaten disappeared..

Meritaten

MONTU-EM-HET
An Egyptian official from an influential Theban family (Dynasty XXV). He married the granddaughter of one of the Nubian kings and became the most important official in Thebes. When the Assyrians invaded Egypt in 665BC, he fled to Nubia with King Tanut-Amun. He returned to Egypt when a new Egyptian dynasty (Dynasty XXVI) was established.

MUTNODJMET
Queen of Egypt (Dynasty XVIII). Daughter of Ay, a courtier who became pharaoh. She married a general called **Horemheb**, who became the next king.

MUWATALLISH
King of the Hittites, who fought the Egyptians under Ramesses II at the Battle of Kadesh in 1284BC.

NAKHT
Official at the court of Tuthmosis IV. Royal astronomer, responsible for producing star charts to show how the seasons affected the earth. His tomb at Thebes is famous for its wall paintings.

NARMER see Menes.

NECHO I (c.672-664BC)
Prince of Sais (Lower Egypt). Necho's family had never accepted the Nubian kings of Dynasty XXV. When the Assyrians invaded Egypt in 664BC Necho sided with them. He was appointed governor by the Assyrians, but was captured and executed by the Nubians. His son Psamtek escaped and returned to restore Egypt's independence as the founder of Dynasty XXVI. However, the Egyptians regarded Necho as the first king of the new dynasty and so he is known as Necho I.

NECTANEBO I (c.379-361BC)
King of Egypt (First ruler of Dynasty XXX). During his reign, the Persians mounted an invasion of Egypt, but had to turn back when the Nile flooded. Peace followed and many monuments were built.

NECTANEBO II (c.359-342BC)
King of Egypt (third and final ruler of Dynasty XXX). After the Persians conquered Egypt, he fled to Memphis, and then to Ethiopia.

NEFERTARI
Chief queen of **Ramesses II** (Dynasty XIX). One of the temples at Abu Simbel was built for her, as well as a tomb in the Valley of the Queens.

NEFERTITI
Queen of Egypt (Dynasty XVIII). Wife of **Akhenaten** and mother of **Akhesenamun**.

Nefertiti

NITOCRIS (or NET-IKERTY)
God's Wife. Daughter of Psamtek I, first king of Dynasty XXVI. She helped reconcile Upper Egypt to the new dynasty.

NITOCRIS
Queen of Egypt (Dynasty VI). Daughter of **Pepi II**. The direct male line appears to have died out soon after her father's death and Nitocris ruled on her own for about two years (c.2152-2150BC).

PEPI II (c.2246-2252BC)
King of Egypt (Dynasty VI). He reigned for 94 years; the longest recorded reign in history. After his death, disputes broke out over the succession. Egypt collapsed into civil conflict and confusion and the Old Kingdom came to an end.

PIANKHI (c.728-716BC)
King of Nubia and Egypt. He saw himself as the guardian of Egyptian culture and religion at a time of decadence and political division in Egypt. Conquered Egypt in 728BC, and became the first king of Dynasty XXV. He died in Nubia and is buried under a pyramid at el Kurru.

PINUDJEM
Egyptian High Priest and Great Commander of the Army. After the death of Ramesses XI, he first recognized the rule of Smendes, but then proclaimed himself king too. Smendes ruled from Tanis, while Pinudjem made Thebes his capital.

PSUSENNES I (c.1039-991BC)
King of Egypt (Dynasty XXI). Known for his tomb at Tanis which was found intact, with a beautiful silver coffin.

PTOLEMY I (305-284BC)
King of Egypt. A general in the army of **Alexander the Great**, he was appointed governor of Egypt after Alexander's death, ruling on behalf of Alexander's son and retarded brother. When they were both murdered, Ptolemy became king and founder of the Ptolemaic dynasty.

RAMESSES II (c.1289-1224BC)
King of Egypt (Dynasty XIX). One of the best known kings in Egyptian history. Ramesses built a large number of fortresses, temples and monuments, including two temples cut into the rock face at Abu Simbel. During the early part of his reign he was engaged in a struggle with the Hittites. Eventually fear of the Assyrians brought an end to the conflict and peace was made between the two sides.

RAMESSES III (c.1184-1153BC)
King of Egypt (Dynasty XX). Son of Set-nakht, he was the last great king of the New Kingdom. He fought the Libyans, overcame an attack by the Sea Peoples, and built a huge mortuary complex at Medinat Habu. His tomb is in the Valley of the Kings and his mummy is in the Cairo Museum.

RAMOSE
Vizier of Upper Egypt during the reigns of **Amenhotep III** and **Akhenaten**. A member of the successful family of **Amenhotep, son of Hapu**.

REKHMIRE
Vizier of Upper Egypt (reign of **Tuthmosis III**). His tomb at Thebes contains valuable scenes of daily life, as well as a text which describes the instructions given by the king to the Vizier on his appointment to office.

SENEFERU (c.2575-2551BC)
King of Egypt (Dynasty III). Son of Huni and a secondary wife, he became king after the early death of the heir. To strengthen his claim, he married his half-sister **Hetepheres I**. Tough, efficient and ruthless, he sent an expedition to Nubia and captured or killed many Nubians. He built himself two pyramids - the 'Bent' Pyramid and the Red Pyramid (the first straight-sided pyramid).

SENNACHERIB (c.704-681BC)
King of Assyria. Son of **Sargon II**. During his reign there were constant revolts in Babylon, led by **Merodach-Baladin**. These ended when the Assyrians sacked Babylon in 689BC. The kings of Sidon, Ashkalon, Judah and Ekron rebelled, encouraged by the King of Egypt. After defeating the rebels, he invaded Egypt, but the Egyptians were saved by the sudden withdrawal of the Assyrian army after an outbreak of the plague. Sennacherib was murdered by one of his sons who crushed him with a statue of a god.

SENUSRET III (c.1878-1841BC)
King of Egypt (Dynasty XII). He led several campaigns against the Kushites who were threatening the frontiers of Nubia (established at the Second Cataract). He also began a huge rebuilding operation, to strengthen the fortresses there, and dug a channel through the First Cataract, so ships could sail directly upstream. He claimed to have established his frontier further south than any previous king.

SHOSHENQ I (c.945-924BC)
King of Egypt. Founder and first king of Dynasty XXII. During his reign, the eastern border was under threat, and he mounted a series of campaigns in Palestine against the states of Israel and Judah. He began ambitious building works, expecially at Karnak. His tomb is at Tanis in the Nile Delta.

SHOSHENQ II (c.890BC)

King of Egypt (Dynasty XXII). Thought to have been co-regent during the period between Osorkon I and Takeloth I. His mummy was found at Tanis in the tomb of **Psusennes I**.

SHUPPILULIUMA (C.1380-1340BC)

The greatest of the Hittite kings, a wily and able ruler and diplomat and a successful soldier. Under him the Hittite empire reached its greatest extent. In about 1370BC he conquered the Mitannian empire and encouraged discontented Egyptian vassals to rebel. When **Tutankhamun** died, his young widow **Ankhesenpaamun** wrote to him, offering to marry one of her sons and make him King of Egypt. Shuppiluliuma eventually sent one of his sons to Egypt, but the plot was discovered and the Hittite prince was murdered. To avenge his son, he attacked Egypt's northern provinces in Syria.

SINUHE

Egyptian army officer (Dynasty XII). On a campaign against the Libyans, he heard that **Amenemhat I** had been murdered, and there was a plot to deprive his son Senusret of the throne. For some unknown reason, Sinuhe fled in panic to Syria, where he stayed for many years. After numerous adventures he returned home. His story is inscribed on the walls of his tomb and was copied and turned into a book.

SOBEK-NEFERU (c.1787-1783BC)

Queen of Egypt (Dynasty XII). With the death of her brother Amenemhat IV the direct male line of Dynasty XII died out and she ruled alone for four years.

TAHARQA (c.690-664BC)

King of Egypt (Dynasty XXV: the Nubian kings). Son of **Piankhi**. The Assyrians attacked Egypt three times during Taharqa's reign. The second invasion reached Memphis, but he escaped to Nubia and later returned. In the third invasion the Assyrians were supported by Egyptian princes such as **Necho of Sais**. Taharka again fled to Nubia, and a new native Egyptian dynasty was established.

TAO II

King of Thebes (Dynasty XVII). Son of Tao I and **Teti-sheri**. During his reign the Thebans began plotting to drive out the Hyksos who were ruling Egypt from Avaris as Dynasty XV. War broke out between them and Tao succeeded in pushing his frontier north to Assyut.

TAWOSRET (c.1194-1186BC)

Queen of Egypt (Dynasty XIX). Daughter of **Merenptah** and sister-wife of Seti II. After Merenptah's death, Amenmesse (a member of the royal family) seized the throne briefly before Seti took control. When Seti died Amenmesse's son Siptah was made ruler. Tawosret married him and when he died she reigned as a "king" until her death three years later.

TETI (c.2323-2291BC)

King of Egypt. Founder of Dynasty VI, he established a claim to the throne through his wife, Queen Ipwet, daughter of King Unas, the last king of Dynasty V. He built a pyramid at Saqqara and was murdered by his guards, in mysterious circumstances.

TETI-SHERI

Queen of Thebes (Dynasty XVII). Wife of Tao I. A woman of great influence, she may have encouraged the men of her family to rebel against the Hyksos. They were driven out by her grandson **Ahmose**, who provided her with Hyksos estates, a burial at Thebes and a monument at Abydos.

THUYA

High Priestess of the god Min, wife of **Yuya** and mother of **Tiy**.

Thuya

TIA

Egyptian princess (Dynasty XIX). Eldest daughter of Seti I and sister of **Ramesses II**. She married a high-ranking official and is buried with him at Saqqara. The marriage probably took place before her grandfather, Ramesses I, founded Dynasty XIX. Otherwise she would probably have married her brother **Ramesses II**.

TIY

Queen of Egypt (Dynasty XVIII). Daughter of two influential courtiers: **Thuya** and **Yuya**. Wife of **Amenhotep III** (who may have also been her cousin) and mother of **Akhenaten**.

TUTANKHAMUN (c.1347-1337BC)

King of Egypt (Dynasty XVIII). Son of **Akhenaten**. He came to the throne aged only about nine and married his half-sister **Ankhesenamun**. A general called **Horemheb** and a courtier called Ay became regents. Although Tutankhamun died young, he is famous because of the treasures found in the 1920s in his tomb in the Valley of the Kings. Many of the tombs of the Dynasty XVIII kings have been repeatedly robbed over the centuries, but Tutankhamun's tomb had escaped attention.

TUTHMOSIS III (c.1490-1436BC)

King of Egypt (Dynasty XVIII). Son of Tuthmosis II and nephew of **Hatshepsut**, was was regent and kept him from power for the last twenty years of his reign. Tuthmosis was probably the greatest of the warrior pharaohs of the New Kingdom. He enlarged the Egyptian empire to its widest limits.

YUYA

Important nobleman at the court of **Amenhotep III**. Vizier of the North and High Priest of Min, he was also in charge of the royal stables and chariots, and of the cattle of the temple of Min. He and his wife **Thuya** have a beautifully furnished tomb at Biban el-Moluk.

GODS AND GODDESSES

The Egyptians worshipped hundreds of gods and goddesses. There were so many of them that it is sometimes difficult to work out which was which. As the Egyptian religion evolved over the centuries, the identities of some early gods disappeared, as they merged together in people's minds, while other gods split up their roles to form separate new gods.

Many gods and goddesses were associated with certain animals, and they were often shown in paintings as that animal or with an animal mask. Major gods, like the sun god, were worshipped throughout Egypt, but some others were local gods, linked to a particular town or temple.

AKER
Aker was the double-lion god, guardian of the sunrise and sunset. Often shown as two lions back-to-back, with the disc of the Sun between them, balanced between the east and west horizons.

AMUN
In his earliest form, Amun was god of air and wind. Later he was worshipped as a fertility god and Creator of all things. In the New Kingdom, Amun became king of the gods and father of all the pharaohs. He was associated with the Sun god Re and so became known as Amun-Re.

Temple: Karnak
Animals: goose and ram

Amun

AMMUT
A female demon. She was known as 'the devourer' and ate the hearts of dead people judged not to have led good lives.

ANUBIS
Anubis was the god of the dead and of magic and embalming. He guided the dead through the darkness of the underworld. He was the son of Osiris and Nepthys.

Animal: jackal

Anubis

ANUKIS
Anukis was the goddess of the First Cataract on the River Nile. She was the daughter of Khnum and Satis.

ATEN
Represented as the Sun's disc with rays, Aten was the Lord of the Heaven and the Earth. He became the most important god during the reign of Akhenaten.

BAST
Bast was a sun and mother goddess. She was the daughter of the sun god Re and represented the life-giving power of the Sun to heal sickness and to ripen the crops.

Temple: Bubastis
Animal: cat

BES
Bes was a dwarf and jester to the gods. He was also the protector of people's homes and of children.

Bes

GEB
Twin brother and husband of Nut, Geb was god of the Earth. He was known as the Great Cackler and often represented as a goose. He was said to have laid the egg from which the Sun was hatched. Father of Osiris, Isis, Seth and Nepthys.

HAPI
God of the Nile, with special responsibility for the annual floods, Hapi was therefore very important to everyone throughout the land. His followers regarded him as even more important than the Sun god.

HATHOR
Hathor, the wife of Horus, was one of the earliest goddesses and was identified with many local goddesses. She was the goddess of love, beauty and joy, and a mother and death goddess.

Temple: Denderah
Animal: cow

Hathor

HORUS
Horus, god of the sky, was said to have inherited the throne of Egypt from Osiris.

Temple: Edfu
Animal: falcon

IHY
Ihy was the god of music and musicians. He was the son of Horus and Hathor.

ISIS
One of the earliest and most important goddesses, Isis was worshipped as the great mother-goddess and goddess of crafts. The daughter of Nut and Geb, she was married to her brother Osiris.

Temple: Philae

KHEPI
A Sun god linked to sunrise, he was often shown as a scarab beetle pushing a dung ball. This was a symbol of the Sun, as Egyptians believed Khepi pushed the Sun across the sky each day.

KHNUM
Khnum was a potter who created people from clay on his potter's wheel. He was believed to control the source of the Nile.

Temple: Elephantine
Animal: ram

KHONSU

Khonsu was the moon god. He was the son of Amun and Mut.

Temple: Karnak

MA'AT

Ma'at was the goddess of truth and justice. She represented the balance and harmony of the universe.

Symbol: feather

MIN

Min was worshipped by men as the god of fertility and later as a rain god who helped crops to grow.

Temple: Coptos
Animal: bull
Plant: lettuce

MITHOS

Mithos was the lion-headed god and son of Bast.

MUT

Mut was a mother goddess and wife of Amun. She was the queen of all gods and the mother of all living things.

Temple: Karnak
Animal: lioness

Mut

NEFERTEM

Nefertem was the god of oils and perfumes. He was the son of Ptah and Sekhmet.

Flower: sacred blue lotus

NEITH

Neith was the goddess of hunting, war and weaving. Later she was worshipped as a protector of the dead and as a guide in the underworld. She was also guardian of the Red Crown of Lower Egypt. She was the mother of the Sun.

Temple: Sais
Symbol: shield and arrows

NEPTHYS

Nepthys was a protector of the dead. She was married to her brother Set, god of deserts.

Ma at

NUT

Nut was goddess of the sky. She was the daughter of Shu and married to her brother Geb, god of the Earth. She is often shown stretching from one horizon to the other, only her fingertips and toes touching the ground. Her husband Geb is often shown stretched out beneath her.

OSIRIS

Egyptians regarded Osiris as King of Egypt. He introduced vines and grain to the land, and became supreme god, judge and ruler of the dead. Son and heir of Geb and Nut, and the symbol of eternal life.

Temple: Abydos

PTAH

Ptah was patron of the city of Memphis, and patron of artists, sculptors and architects. He was himself an architect and was responsible for building the framework of the universe.

Temple: Memphis
Animal: Apis bull

RE

Re was the most common form of the Sun god, although there were many different versions. Each day Re was born again and began a journey across the sky.

Temple: Heliopolis

RENENUTET

Renenutet, a protector of children, was a goddess of great powers. Her gaze could destroy her enemies, but it could also make crops and livestock grow and fatten.

Temple: Medinet el Fayum
Animal: snake

SATIS

Satis was patroness of hunters. As guardian of Egypt's southern border with Nubia, she was responsible for killing the pharaoh's enemies. She was married to Khnum.

SEKHMET

Sekhmet represented motherhood and the burning, destructive power of the Sun. A fierce goddess of war, she was the wife of Ptah and the daughter of Nut and Geb.

Animal: lioness

SET

Set was god of deserts and trouble, also known as Lord of Upper Egypt. Son of Geb and Nut, he was Osiris's evil brother. Set killed Osiris, and took his place on the throne of Egypt. Later dynasties worshipped Set as a protector from desert storms. He was married to his sister Nepthys.

Animals: donkey, pig and hippopotamus

SHU

Shu was the god of atmosphere and of dry winds. He was the son of Re, brother and husband of Tefnut, and the father of Geb and Nut.

SOBEK

Sobek was the god of water, and admired but feared for his ferocity. Often shown with the head of a crocodile. Husband of Renenutet.

Sobek

Temples: Faiyum and Kom Ombo
Animal: crocodile

TAWERET

Taweret was a female hippopotamus. She was the goddess of childbirth and was responsible for looking after pregnant women and babies.

THOTH

Thoth was the moon god and god of wisdom. His role was to be vizier and scribe to all the gods and was keeper and recorder of all knowledge. He was married to Ma'at.

Temple: Hermopolis
Animal: baboon
Bird: ibis

Tawaret

THE HISTORY OF EGYPTOLOGY

Egyptology means the study of the history and archaeology of ancient Egypt. Egypt was the world's first tourist destination. The Egyptian monuments were the object of awe and admiration - and of plunder too - almost from the moment they were first constructed. Many of Egypt's conquerors - the Greeks, the Romans and the Arabs - studied the ancient ruins with great interest, and the country attracted visitors from other parts of the Mediterranean as well.

But it was not until late in the 19th century that European archaeologists began introducing scientific methods of excavation, which dramatically improved our understanding of Egyptian civilization. Here are some of the landmarks in the history of Egyptology.

Great Sphinx and pyramids of Giza by David Roberts, a Scottish artist who journeyed to Egypt in 1838. His paintings of the great monuments did much to encourage European interest in the subject.

c.500BC Greek historian Herodotus visited Egypt and made the first record of Egyptian history and civilization by a foreigner. But his account was mainly based on what people told him, so some of it was myth rather than fact.

Herodotus, the Greek historian, known as the "father of history"

c.290BC An Egyptian priest named Manetho wrote the *History of Egypt* for Pharaoh Ptolemy II. This divided Egypt's history into 30 dynasties, a system which is still used today.

c.59BC Greek writer Diodorus Siculus wrote a 12-volume Universal History. The last volume dealt with the history and customs of Egypt.

25BC Roman geographer named Strabo visited Egypt. He wrote the 17-volume *Geographia* which included information on Egyptian tombs, temples and pyramids.

c.AD50 Roman historian Pliny the Elder was the first Roman to describe the Great Sphinx at Giza. He made records of the monuments in Egypt, and of those brought out of Egypt to Rome, such as obelisks.

AD378-388 A Christian nun known as Lady Etheria from Gaul (France) voyaged to Egypt and described the monuments around Thebes.

c. AD1200 Arab doctor Abd' el-Latif from Baghdad visited Giza, entered the Great Pyramid and saw the Great Sphinx. He wrote that the word 'mummy' comes from the Persian term *moumiya,* meaning pitch or bitumen.

1646 John Greaves, Professor of anatomy at Oxford University, wrote *Pyramidographia*. This tried to find the real purpose of the pyramids, comparing the facts with the stories that had grown up around them.

1657 French voyager Jean de Thevenot wrote about his journey to Egypt in a book called *Voyage au Levant.*

1692 Benoit de Maillot, French consul in Egypt, explored the Great Pyramid at Giza and argued for scientific exploration of Egypt and its monuments.

Between **1707** and **1726** Jesuit priest Claude Sicard voyaged around Egypt. He went as far south as Aswan, recording monuments and collecting information on 20 pyramids, 24 temples and over 50 decorated tombs. This was the most extensive coverage at that time. His most important work was to identify the temples at Karnak and Luxor as part of the ancient capital at Thebes.

1755 Frederick Nordern, Danish engineer and artist, published a book called *Voyage*. This gave a detailed description of Egypt with accurate plans and drawings of many of the monuments.

1768 Scottish explorer James Bruce sailed up the Nile and discovered the tomb of Ramesses III in the Valley of the Kings.

1798 Napoleon Bonaparte arrived in Egypt with an invading army and defeated the Egyptians at the Battle of the Pyramids. But he had also brought scholars with him to collect information about Egypt.

Various members of this commission stayed for three years and worked in different parts of the country, mapping and collecting information about its natural history, ancient monuments and the customs of the people. The books that were published made a huge impact in Europe and served as the foundation for modern Egyptology.

1799 The Rosetta Stone was discovered by French soldiers at Fort Rachid near Rosetta in Egypt. A large slab of basalt containing identical texts in Greek, Egyptian hieratic and hieroglyphics, it later provided the clue to deciphering the mystery of Egyptian hieroglyphs.

1815 English physician Thomas Young published *Remarks on Egyptian Papyri and on the Inscription of Rosetta*. This was a vital step towards the deciphering Egyptian hieroglyphs.

1815 Henry Salt was appointed British consul-general in Egypt and collected a number of ancient Egyptian works of art for British museums. He employed Giovanni Battista Belzoni to help him. Belzoni sent back many pieces that are now in the British Museum in London, including the colossal head of Ramesses II from Thebes. He also explored the temples at Abu Simbel, opened up many tombs in the Valley of the Kings and the pyramid of Chephren at Giza, and discovered the ancient port of Berenice on the Red Sea.

1821 John Wilkinson sailed to Egypt and spent the next three years there. He is often

A portrait of Giovanni Belzoni, the Italian treasure hunter

described as the founder of Egyptology in Britain. Wilkinson excavated tombs at Thebes, and his copies of paintings and inscriptions are still among the best ever made.

1824 French scholar Jean François Champollion published *Précis du Système Hiéroglyphique*. This built on Thomas Young's work and finally unlocked the secret of hieroglyphics.

1824 Scottish scholar Robert Hay made drawings, plans and copies of inscriptions on Egyptian monuments.

1825 English physician Augustus Granville performed a scientific autopsy on a mummy named Irtyersenu, showing how much could be learned from mummies.

1834 Italian adventurer Guiseppe Ferlini found a collection of gold jewels in the tomb of Queen Amanishakheto (1st century BC) at Meroë: the largest collection of Meroitic jewellery ever found.

1840s German scholar Karl Lepsius and his team of draftsmen made numerous recordings of drawings and inscriptions from temples and tombs in the Valley of the Kings.

The Egyptian Museum in Cairo, founded by Auguste Mariette, has the largest collection of Egyptian antiquities in the world.

1850s onwards Scottish scholar Henry Rhind set up new methods for excavation, in contrast to the "treasure hunting" that had been conducted so far. He spent two years excavating tombs at Thebes, recording for the first time the precise location of each find.

1858 French archaeologist Auguste Mariette was appointed the first director of ancient monuments in Egypt and head of the new museum near Cairo, the first national museum in the Middle East. He also set up the world's first national antiquities service. From this point on, most of the objects excavated were kept in Egypt rather than taken away to foreign museums. The Cairo Museum now contains the world's largest Egyptian collection.

1871 A family of local treasure-hunters discovered a tomb at Deir el Bahri, containing 36 mummies belonging to members of New Kingdom royal families.

1873 Amelia Edwards, an English writer, made the long journey up the Nile, inspiring many others to follow. She became a founder member of the Egypt Exploration Fund, established in **1882**.

1884 English archaeologist William Flinders Petrie began excavating in Egypt for the British Egypt Exploration Fund. Over a period of 40 years, he made many important discoveries, but his most significant contribution was in introducing scientific methods for the recording of archaeological finds. He introduced stratigraphy (the study of the relative positions of rock strata) and 'sequence dating', for dating and arranging material. His best known digs include Naucratis, a Greek city in Egypt, and Kahun and Gurob, which increased experts' knowledge of daily life in towns. He also studied the famous Amarna Letters ~ found by a peasant woman in a field ~ which revealed new information about Akhenaten.

1893 Farmers stumbled across over 300 fragments of papyrus from the pyramid complex of 5th dynasty King Neferirkare at Abusir. These papyri provided archaeologists with information about the staff, duties and equipment in Egyptian temples.

1898 French archaeologist Victor Loret discovered 13 more royal mummies in Amenhotep II's tomb in the Valley of the Kings.

1898 English archaeologist James Quibell found the palette of King Narmer at Hierakonpolis: a major record of the unification of Egypt.

1913-1914 A German expedition led by Ludwig Borchardt uncovered the house of sculptor Thutmose at Amarna, containing the famous bust of Nefertiti.

1917 A French archaeological expedition began work at Deir el Medina, which led to the discovery of the royal workmen's village.

1919-1920 Herbert Winlock excavated the tomb of Meket-Re in Thebes. Inside were models of the man's house and workshops, giving a detailed glimpse of life at the time.

1922 Howard Carter, backed by Lord Carnarvon, discovered the tomb of King Tutankhamun containing its fabulous treasure.

1920s-1940s Egyptian archaeologist Sami Gabra excavated the human and animal cemeteries at the site of Tuna el-Gebel in Middle Egypt.

1930s Pierre Montet uncovered spectacular treasures from the royal burials of the little-known 21st and 22nd dynasties at Tanis.

1936-1956 William Emery excavated mastaba tombs of 1st and 2nd dynasty officials at Saqqara.

1954 A dismantled and perfectly preserved 4th dynasty funerary ship was found in a large pit south of the Great Pyramid at Giza. It had been buried for 4,600 years.

1960s UNESCO funded an international rescue operation to move the temples at Abu Simbel, so they would not be flooded by the building of a dam at Aswan.

1966 onwards Excavations in the Nile Delta, led by Austrian archaeologist Manfred Bietak, found the Hyksos capital of Avaris and Ramesses II's city at Per Ramesses.

1975 onwards The Akhenaten Temple Project uncovered blocks from Akhenaten's destroyed temples at Amarna, which are being slowly reconstructed.

1978 Hierakonpolis Expedition uncovered the charred remains of a potter's house, providing vital information about Egyptian life in about 3500BC. In **1985,** the remains of Egypt's earliest known temple were uncovered at the same site.

1995 American archaeologist Kent Weeks discovered the huge family tomb of Ramesses II in the Valley of the Kings. It contains at least 118 rooms, most identified by sonar as they were filled with rubble.

1996 Underwater archaeologists led by Franck Goddio started recovering remains of the city of Alexandria, now submerged under the sea, and nearby cities of Canopus, Herakleion and Menouthis, destroyed by earthquake in AD746.

1999 At least 200 mummies, some with gold masks, were discovered at Bawati in the Western Desert, dating from the early Graeco-Roman era. The burial ground, thought to contain over 10,000 mummies, may be the biggest ever found.

1999 An Egyptian-German team uncovered some of the world's oldest stables on the edge of the Nile Delta. Housing up to 460 horses, they are the biggest stables ever found in the ancient Middle East and have been linked to Pharaoh Ramesses II.

2000-2001 Important underwater archeological finds at Herakleion, in the Bay of Aboukir, include colossal statues, a stela with an inscription of Nectanebo I, a Ptolemaic shrine to Amun, and the remains of 10 ancient Egyptian ships.

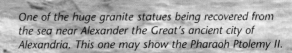

One of the huge granite statues being recovered from the sea near Alexander the Great's ancient city of Alexandria. This one may show the Pharaoh Ptolemy II.

EGYPTIAN COLLECTIONS

You don't have to visit Egypt to see great works of Ancient Egyptian art and architecture. You can find amazing collections of Egyptian paintings, sculpture, furniture, pottery, jewels and other treasures in museums all over the world.

Here is a list of some of the best ones. Many of them also have Web sites, so you can look at part of their collections on line, without even leaving home. For links to the Web sites of many of the museums described on the next three pages, go to **www.usborne-quicklinks.com** and type in the keywords **Ancient Egypt**.

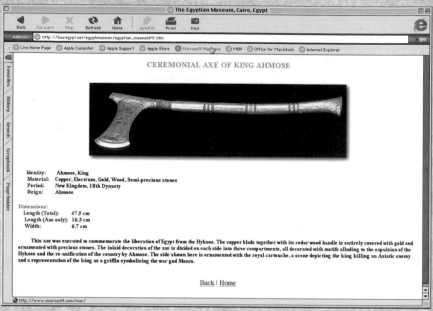

The Egyptian Museum in Cairo has everything from coins to sarcophagi on display.

AUSTRALIA

Museum of Ancient Cultures
Macquarie University
Sydney
New South Wales 2109

AUSTRIA

Kunsthistorisches Museum
Burgring 5
A-1010 Wien

The Egypt and Near Eastern collection in this great museum is one of the best in the world. Begun in the 19th century, it has grown through purchases, donations and new acquisitions from excavations.

Papyrussammlung Osterreichische Nationalbibliothek
Josefsplatz 1
A-1010 Wien

One of the most important libraries in Austria, with a huge collection of books, manuscripts, including Egyptian papyri.

BELGIUM

Musée Royal de Mariemont
Section Égypt et Proche Orient
Chaussée de Mariemont, 100
B-7410 Morlanwelz

Musées Royaux d'Art et d'Histoire
Collection égyptienne
10, Parc du Cinquantenaire
B-1000 Bruxelles

Contains more than 11,000 pieces, from all periods of Egyptian history.

CANADA

Royal Ontario Museum
100 Queen's Park
Toronto, Ontario M5S 2C6

EGYPT

The Egyptian Museum
Midan el-Tahrir
Cairo

Founded in 1858, this was the first national museum in the Middle East, and houses the greatest collection of Egyptian antiquities in the world.

FRANCE

Musée du Louvre
75058 Paris Cedex 01

The Egyptian Museum at the Louvre opened in 1827. It was founded by Jean-François Champollion, and was based on the collections of the British and French consuls in Egypt. One of the best and most comprehensive collections of Egyptian antiquities.

The Louvre Web site has photographs of many of their best treasures.

GERMANY

Äegyptisches Museum
Schillerstr. 6
04109 Leipzig

Äegyptisches Museum und Papyrussammlung
Bodenstr. 1-3
10178 Berlin

GREECE

National Archaeological Museum
Patission Street 44
106 82 Athens

The most important archaeological museum in Greece. Completed in 1889, it houses an extensive collection of ancient Egyptian art.

IRELAND

National Museum of Ireland
Collins Barracks, Benburb St.
Dublin 7

ITALY

Archaeological Museum
Via dell' Archiginnasio, 2
Bologna

Museo Gregoriano Egiziano
Vatican Museum
Rome

NETHERLANDS

Rijksmuseum van Oudheden
Rapenburg 28
P.O.Box 11114
2301 EC Leiden

Re-opened after modernisation, this museum contains an excellent collection of Egyptian art and offers regular tours, lectures and films.

PORTUGAL

Museu Gulbenkian
Av. de Berna 45a
1067-001 Lisboa

This museum houses the collection of Turkish-born industrialist Calouste Gulbenkian (1865-1955).

UNITED KINGDOM

Ashmolean Museum
Beaumont Street
Oxford OX1 2PH

A wide-ranging collection of Egyptian art, based on its long association with Egyptologists.

Hunterian Museum and Art Gallery
University of Glasgow
Glasgow G12 8QQ

This museum, which opened in 1807, is part of Glasgow university. It is the oldest public museum in Scotland and contains an excellent of Egyptian art.

The British Museum displays include a famous collection of Egyptian mummies and coffins.

British Museum
Great Russell Street
London WC1B 3DG

The British Museum houses one of the most important collections of Egyptian antiquities outside Egypt. It covers every aspect of Egyptian culture, from the Predynastic Period to the Coptic Christian Period, and is especially well known for its collection of mummies.

Durham University Oriental Museum
School of Oriental Studies
Elvet Hill Road, Durham DH1 3TH

Fitzwilliam Museum
Trumpington Street
Cambridge CB1 1RD

INTERNET LINK

Go to **www.usborne-quicklinks.com**
for links to the Web sites of museums with collections of Egyptian art.

On the Rijksmuseum Web site, you can see a 3-D reconstruction of an Egyptian temple.

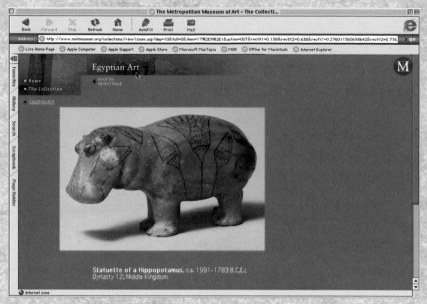

Egyptian Art

Statuette of a Hippopotamus, ca. 1991–1783 B.C.E.;
Dynasty 12; Middle Kingdom

*This blue faience hippopotamus is one of the many Middle Kingdom tomb models
you can see online on the Metropolitan Museum of Art Web site.*

INTERNET LINK

Go to **www.usborne-quicklinks.com**
*for links to the Web sites of museums
with collections of Egyptian art.*

The Manchester Museum
University of Manchester
Oxford Road
Manchester M13 9PL

One of the best collections in the
world of objects from daily life in
Ancient Egypt. An Egyptian Mummy
Research Project has been based
there since 1973.

**The Petrie Museum of
Egyptian Archaeology**
University College
Gower Street
London WC1E 6BT

With about 80,000 ancient Egyptian
and Sudanese objects in its
collection, this is one of the largest
in the world. It is named after the
great archaeologist William Flinders
Petrie (1853-1942).

Wellcome Museum
Department of Classics and
Ancient History
University of Wales Swansea
Singleton Park
Swansea SA2 8P

The main collection of Egyptian
antiquities in Wales and one of the
main bases of Egyptology in the U.K.

U.S.A.

Boston Museum of Fine Arts
465, Huntington Avenue
Boston
Massachusetts 02115-5523

One of the most important museums
of North America, its collection of
Egyptian antiquities began in 1872.
Many of its most famous exhibits
were found during excavations at
Giza in the early 20th century.

**Carnegie Museum of Natural
History**
4400 Forbes Avenue
Pittsburgh
Pennsylvania 15213

Visit the Walton Hall of Ancient
Egypt inside the Museum for a
exhibition of life in Ancient Egypt.

Cleveland Museum of Art
University Circle
11150 East Boulevard
Cleveland
Ohio 44106-1797

The **Cleveland Museum of Art
Web site** has a special children's
section – **Rosetta Stone's Pharaoh
Adventure –** with quizzes and
drawings to fill in, and a pharaoh's
mask to cut out and make.

Detroit Institute of Arts
5200 Woodward Avenue
Detroit
Michigan 48202

This museum has an excellent
collection of items from all over the
ancient Mediterranean.

**Institute of Egyptian Art and
Archaeology**
3750 Norriswood Avenue
Memphis
Tennessee 38152

The Field Museum
1400 S.Lake Shore Drive
Chicago
Illinois 60605-2496

Metropolitan Museum of Art
1000 Fifth Avenue
New York
NY 10028

The treasures of this great museum's
Egyptian collection include an Old
Kingdom mastaba, Middle Kingdom
tomb models, and jewels belonging
to a 12th dynasty princess.

Michael C.Carlos Museum
Emory University
571 Kilgo Street
Atlanta
Georgia 30322

As well as showing the development
of Egyptian civilization, the New
Egyptian Collection includes other
works from ancient Africa, including
a Nubian gallery.

Oriental Institute Museum
1155 East 58th Street
Chicago
Illinois 60637

Seattle Art Museum
Downtown
100 University Street
Seattle
Washington 98101-2902

GLOSSARY

This glossary explains some of the Egyptian words and specialist words that you may come across in this book, or when reading elsewhere about ancient Egypt. If a word used in an entry has a separate entry of its own, it is shown in *italic* type.

akh One of the three aspects of a person's spirit.

alabaster A translucent, white stone, veined rather like marble. It was used for decorative features, such as floors in temples, and for items such as vases and lamps in wealthy Egyptian households.

amulet A small figure of a god or goddess or a sacred object. Amulets were worn as charms for luck and protection by the living and the dead. Examples include the *djed* pillar, and the scarab beetle.

ankh An Egyptian *amulet* shaped a little like a cross; the symbol of life.

apis bull A sacred bull associated with the god Ptah, who lived at his temple in Memphis. When the apis bull died, there was a nationwide search to identify his successor.

aqueduct A man-made channel for transporting water.

Arab A member of a group of Semitic people living in Arabia and surrounding territory.

Aryan A term used to refer to the language or people of the Iranian and Indian branches of the Indo-European group.

Assyrian A Semitic people from the area around the cities of Ashur and Nineveh on the river Tigris, who built up a huge empire in the Middle East. The Assyrians invaded Egypt during the Third Intermediate Period and brought an end to Nubian rule.

atef crown A tall crown, adorned with ostrich feathers, worn by the pharaoh for religious ceremonies.

ba A person's life force, one of the three aspects of a person's spirit. Thought to survive after death, so long as the body was preserved.

barque A sailing ship.

bedouin *Nomads* inhabiting the deserts of North Africa and Arabia.

caravan A group of people, usually merchants, travelling together for safety across a desert.

cataract A place where large rocks block the path of a river such as the Nile. Cataracts often formed important territorial boundaries in ancient times.

city state A self governing city with its surrounding territory, forming the basis for an independent state.

concubine A term applied in a historical context to a woman who lived with a man without being married. In ancient Egypt it was an officially recognized relationship and a concubine had special rights.

corvée The tax imposed by the pharaohs on Egyptians, which involved giving their time to work on royal building projects.

cubit Egyptian measurement, based on the distance from elbow to fingertip. Seven hands, each four fingers wide, equalled one cubit. Each cubit was divided into digits, finger-widths.

cult The worship of a particular god or goddess, or the following of a particular system of religious rites. Most Egyptian deities had a home town where their main temple, or **cult temple**, was sited. It was the home of the **cult statue**, the means by which the god communicated.

demotic A type of shorthand Egyptian script that evolved during the Late Period.

djed pillar An Egyptian *amulet* representing stability and continuity of power.

dowry Money or property brought by a woman to her husband at the time of marriage.

dynasty A succession of hereditary rulers. Dynasties are often referred to by a family name. Egyptian dynasties are numbered I to XXXI.

electrum A naturally occuring alloy (mixture) of gold and silver.

exile Enforced absence from a home or country.

faience A type of glazed earthenware, made by heating powdered quartz (a type of rock).

God's Wife Head of the priestesses at the temple of Amun at Karnak. By the Third Intermediate Period this was a very powerful position held by a princess.

harem The name given to the part of an Oriental (often Muslim) house reserved strictly for women (wives and *concubines*). The part of an ancient Egyptian palace where the royal women lived.

Heb Sed An Egyptian festival, at which the king had to perform certain physical activities, including a ceremonial run, to demonstrate to the people that he was still at the height of his powers.

Hebrew An ancient Semitic language and people. The people are also known as *Israelites* and Jews, and the language is spoken today in Israel.

heretic A person who maintains a set of beliefs condemned by the established religion. The beliefs held by a heretic are described as **heretical** and the person is said to be guilty of **heresy**.

hieratic An Egyptian shorthand script developed in the Old Kingdom, used mainly by priests.

hieroglyphics The Egyptian system of writing in which pictures or signs are used to represent objects, ideas or sounds. The pictures themselves are known as **hieroglyphs** The word comes from the Greek for 'sacred sculptures'. The Egyptians themselves called them 'words of the god' after the god Thoth who was thought to have introduced writing.

Hittites An *Indo-European* people from Anatolia (in modern Turkey), who built up a great empire in Asia Minor and northern Syria in the second millennium BC.

Hyksos A group of Semitic peoples, probably mostly nomads, who invaded and conquered Egypt during the Second Intermediate Period.

hypostyle hall The central hall in a Egyptian temple, surounded by tall columns.

Indo-European A group of languages which includes Iranian, Armenian and Sanskrit (the ancient literary language of India), as well as most modern European languages. The name is also given to those groups of people speaking early Indo-European languages who drifted into the Middle East in about 2000BC. They may have originated in the area that stretches from southern Russia to central Europe.

inundation The usual term for the annual flooding of the Nile. Every spring, rain and snow in the highlands of Ethiopia sent a huge quantity of water down the Nile, reaching Egypt by about July. The river overflowed and flooded its banks, depositing silt, a rich fertile mud, on its banks. The Egyptians developed a sophisticated irrigation system to make use of the floodwater. As a result, they built up a successful farming economy, which ultimately provided the basis for their civilization.

Israelites The *Hebrew* inhabitants of the Kingdom of **Israel**.

Jews Another name for the Semitic people also known as *Israelites* and *Hebrews*; people who follow the religion **Judaism**.

ka A person's spirit double, one of the three aspects of a person's spirit. Thought to survive after death, so long as the body was preserved.

khephresh A bright blue crown worn by the pharaoh. More of a battle helmet than a crown, it reflected the importance of the king's role as a warrior.

Kush A kingdom in southern Nubia, situated around the 3rd Cataract of the Nile. During the New Kingdom, the Egyptians invaded and occupied Nubia, and appointed a viceroy, known as the King's Son of Kush, to rule over the region.

Libyans A people from a land to the west of Egypt, who at various times attempted to invade or settle in Egypt. At the end of the New Kingdom, Libyan settlers in the Nile Delta established themselves as rulers, forming the 22nd dynasty.

mastaba A brick building containing tombs, used for Egyptian royal burials before the introduction of pyramids.

Medjay The name of a Nubian tribe some of whose members came to Egypt as mercenary soldiers. The role of the Medjay later evolved into that of a peace-keeping force, and the term was also applied to native Egyptians who joined it.

mercenary A man who is paid to fight in a foreign army.

millennium One thousand years. The first millennium BC means the thousand year period immediately before the birth of Christ.

miracle A wonderful event which cannot be explained by natural causes and is attributed to divine intervention.

mortuary A building where dead bodies are placed before burial. The Egyptian kings had **mortuary temples** attached to their pyramids and tombs.

mummy An embalmed body ready for burial. Over time, the oils and resins used in the wrapping stage of the embalming process became thick and sticky, almost like tar. The Arabic word for this substance was *moumiya*, meaning 'bitumen' (tar is made partly of bitumen). So, this is the origin of the word 'mummy'.

naos The inner sanctuary at the back of a temple, where the statue of the god was kept.

necropolis A cemetery.

Next World The place where Egyptians thought people lived after death.

niche A recess in a wall, especially one that contains a statue.

nomads People who do not live permanently in any one area, but move from place to place. People who live in this way are described as **nomadic**.

nome The Greek name for an Egyptian administrative district. Each nome was governed by an official, or governor, called a **nomarch**.

Nubians People from the land south of Egypt (now Sudan). The Egyptians conquered Nubia during the New Kingdom, but were ruled by Nubian pharaohs of the 25th dynasty during the Third Intermediate Period.

obelisk A stone pillar, erected as a monument to the sun god, with flat sides that taper towards a pyramid-shaped top.

omen A sign from the gods, such as shooting stars, which warned of good or evil to come. Priests were specially trained to interpret omens.

oracle A message from a god or goddess. In Egypt it was usually communicated through a cult statue or a sacred animal, in response to questions posed by priests on behalf of their worshippers. People consulted the oracle in order to find solutions to personal problems and fears. Kings also used it in an attempt to acquire divine approval for their policies.

ostraca (singular: **ostracon**) Pieces of broken pottery or stone, used for drawing or writing on.

overlord A supreme lord or ruler, who has power over other, lesser rulers.

papyrus A reed used to make a form of writing material (also called papyrus). The reed was cut into strips, which were pressed and dried to make a smooth writing surface.

patron Someone who sponsors or helps another person, usually by providing money or a job.

pectoral An ornament, often decorated with jewels, worn on the chest on a chain.

Phrygians An *Indo-European* people from Phrygia, an ancient kingdom in Asia Minor.

pylon The main gateway to an Egyptian temple.

regent Someone who rules in the place of the actual ruler who is either absent, incapable or still too young to take power.

relief A sculpture carved on a flat background. Raised reliefs were made by cutting away the background and modelling details on to the figures. Sunken, or bas, reliefs were made by cutting away stone from inside the outlines of the figures and carving the details out of the body.

Romans A people from the city of Rome in central Italy, founded in the 8th century BC, which became the heart of a great civilization. The Romans built up a huge empire in Europe and around the Mediterranean, conquering Egypt in 30BC. Their empire reached its greatest extent in the 1st century AD and declined in the 4th century AD, but its cultural influence continues to the present day.

sacrifice A gift or offering made to a deity by people of early civilizations. This sometimes consisted of fruit, vegetables or flowers, but it could also involve the ritual killing of animals and humans.

sarcophagus A stone coffin or tomb, often decorated with inscriptions or carvings.

scribe A person specifically employed to write and copy texts and keep records. This was a highly regarded profession in ancient times, when relatively few people could read and write. Scribes were eligible for well-paid and prestigious jobs in government.

Sea Peoples The name given to various groups of peoples who migrated to places around the eastern Mediterranean in around 1190BC. They tried to invade Egypt and became involved in battles with the Egyptians on land and at sea, particularly during the reign of Ramesses III. Although Ramesses defeated them, Egypt was weakened by the conflict and soon lost much of its empire.

Second Cataract The frontier between Egypt and Nubia in the Middle Kingdom. The site of the great Middle Kingdom fortresses.

Seleucid A dynasty and kingdom founded by Seleucus Nicator, a Macedonian general under Alexander the Great. In 304BC, the Seleucids seized a large part of Alexander's empire, but it proved impossible to hold together. Large areas began to break away. In 64BC Seleucid lands were conquered by the *Romans* and incorporated into the Roman empire.

Semites Groups of people who, in about 2500BC, occupied an area which stretched from northern Mesopotamia to the eastern borders of Egypt. The Semites spoke closely related dialects which form part of the language group known by modern scholars as Semitic. Early Semites include the Akkadians and the Babylonians. Jews and Arabs are modern Semites.

shrine This is both a temple where a deity is worshipped and a container made of wood, stone or precious metal in which the figure of a god or goddess is kept.

shroud A rectangular piece of cloth used to enclose a dead body.

sphinx An Egyptian statue representing the sun god. A sphinx usually had the body of an animal with the head of a lion, ram or pharaoh.

stela (plural: **stelae**) An upright rectangular stone slab (sometimes curved at the top), carved with inscriptions. They were used to commemorate special events and put in tombs to record details about the dead person.

terracotta A mixture of clay and sand, used to make titles and small statues. The statues themselves are sometimes called terracottas.

tribute A payment in money or kind made by a ruler or state to another, as an acknowledgement of submission. A *vassal* pays tribute to an *overlord*.

udjat-eye The eye of Horus, an *amulet* used for healing.

Underworld Another name for the *Next World*, the kingdom of the god Osiris, ruler of the dead. Sometimes known as the Kingdom of the West, because it was thought to be somewhere in the far west.

vassal A subject people who pay *tribute* to a ruler or conqueror.

vizier Chief advisor to the pharaoh. There were two viziers: one in charge of Upper Egypt, the other in charge of Lower Egypt.

wepet renpet Egyptian New Year, coinciding with the date when the star Sirius (known as *sopdet*) sank below the horizon each year, just before the Nile began to rise. The earliest Egyptian calendar was based on the stars. Another was based on the cycle of the moon. The first calendar to divide the year into 365 days was introduced early in the Old Kingdom, possibly by Imhotep. When Julius Caesar visited Egypt, he was so impressed that he took it back to Rome and adapted it. The Julian calendar, as it was known, was used until the 16th century.

INDEX

ACKNOWLEDGEMENTS

Every effort has been made to trace the copyright holders of material in this book. If any rights have been omitted, the publishers offer their sincere apologies and will rectify this in any subsequent editions, following notification. The publishers are grateful to the following individuals and organizations for their permission to reproduce material on the following pages (t = top, m = middle, b = bottom, l = left, r = right, wp = whole page):

end papers ©Historical Picture Archive/CORBIS; **title page** ©Neil Beer/CORBIS; **p2** Art Directors & TRIP/Helene Rogers; **p6** (b) ©Copyright The British Museum, (tr) ©Jim Zuckerman/CORBIS; **p7** (bl, mt) Photo Peter Clayton, (br) The Petrie Museum of Egyptian Archaeology, University College London; **p8** (l) Photo Scala, Florence, (tr) ©Werner Forman Archive: Egyptian Museum, Cairo, (b) The Griffith Institute, Oxford; **p9** ©Gianni Dagli Orti/CORBIS; **pp8-9** ©Robert Holmes/CORBIS; **p10** (tl, tr) ©Dave Bartruff/CORBIS, (l) Photo Peter Clayton, (b) Photo Scala, Florence; **p11** (bl) ©Ludovic Maisant/CORBIS, (r) ©Otto Lang/CORBIS; **pp10-11** ©Historical Picture Archive/CORBIS; **p12** Popperfoto/Reuters; **p15** ©Archivo Iconografico, S. A./CORBIS; **p16** Brooklyn Museum of Art, Museum Collection Fund 07.447.505; **p17** (bl) ©Werner Forman Archive: Egyptian Museum, Cairo, (b) Digital image ©1996 CORBIS: Original image courtesy of NASA/CORBIS; **p18** (tl) ©Charles and Josette Lenars/CORBIS, (t) ©Copyright The British Museum, (b) ©Michael Nicholson/CORBIS; **p19** (tl) Photo Scala, Florence, (m) ©Roger Wood/CORBIS, (r) ©Charles and Josette Lenars/CORBIS; **p20** ©Gianni Dagli Orti/CORBIS; **p23** ©Archivo Iconografico, S.A./CORBIS; **pp22-23** (b) ©Michael Nicholson/CORBIS; **p24** Photo Scala, Florence; **p25** (t) ©Carmen Redondo/CORBIS, (m) ©O. Alamany & E. Vicens/CORBIS; **p26** (tl) ©Gianni Dagli Orti/CORBIS, (l) ©Richard T. Norwitz/CORBIS; **p27** ©Gianni Dagli Orti/CORBIS; **p28** (bl) ©Archivo Iconografico, S. A./CORBIS, (m) ©Roger Wood/CORBIS; **p29** (t) Ashmolean Museum, University of Oxford, (b) ©Archivo Iconografico, S. A./CORBIS, (mr) ©Gianni Dagli Orti/CORBIS; **p30** ©Gianni Dagli Orti/CORBIS; **p31** ©Gianni Dagli Orti/CORBIS; **pp30-31** ©Charles and Josette Lenars/CORBIS; **p33** Photo Peter Clayton; **p34** (tl, mr) ©Roger Wood/CORBIS, (bl) The Ancient Egypt Picture Library; **p36** (tl, bl) ©Copyright The British Museum, (ml) ©North Carolina Museum of Art/CORBIS; **p37** (t) ©Araldo de Luca/CORBIS, (b) ©Adam Woolfitt/CORBIS, (wp) Digital Vision; **p38** (b) ©North Carolina Museum of Art/CORBIS, (br) ©Bettman/CORBIS; **p39** Photo Scala, Florence; **p40** ©Gianni Dagli Orti/CORBIS; **p42** (tl, l) ©Roger Wood/CORBIS, (b) ©Copyright The British Museum; **p44** Photo Scala, Florence; **p45** (tr) ©Dr E. Strouhal, (bl) The Ancient Egypt Picture Library; **p46** The Art Archive/Egyptian Museum Cairo/Dagli Orti (A); **p47** ©Copyright The British Museum; **p48** Photo Scala, Florence; **p49** ©Copyright The British Museum; **p52** ©Gianni Dagli Orti/CORBIS; **p54** ©Christine Osborne/CORBIS; **p56** ©Yann Arthus-Bertrand/CORBIS; **p58** ©Copyright the British Museum; **p59** ©Copyright The British Museum; **p60** (tl, b) Vanni Archive/CORBIS, (l) Photo Scala, Florence, (tr) ©Copyright the British Museum; **p61** ©Copyright The British Museum; **p62** ©Bettman/CORBIS; **p63** (l) Ancient Art and Architecture, (r) ALEXANDER TSIARAS/SCIENCE PHOTO LIBRARY, (br) ©THE TRUSTEES OF THE NATIONAL MUSEUMS OF SCOTLAND; **p64** ©Gianni Dagli Orti/CORBIS; **p65** (tl) ©Burnstein Collection/CORBIS, (m) ©Copyright The British Museum, (br) ©Charles and Josette Lenars/CORBIS; **p66** ©Yann Arthus-Bertrand/CORBIS; **p68** ©Roger Wood/CORBIS; **p69** (tl) ©Werner Forman Archive/CORBIS, (bl) ©Gianni Dagli Orti/CORBIS, (br) ©Roger Wood/CORBIS; **pp68-69** Powerstock Zefa; **p70** (tl) ©Roger Wood/CORBIS, (m) ©Eye Ubiquitous/CORBIS; **p71** (tl) ©Vanni Archive/CORBIS, (br) ©Roger Wood/CORBIS; **p72** (m) ©Nik Wheeler/CORBIS, (b) ©Carmen Redondo/CORBIS; **p73** ©Gianni Dagli Orti/CORBIS; **p75** (ml, b) ©Copyright The British Museum, (tr) ©Gianni Dagli Orti/CORBIS; **p76** (tl) ©Burstein Collection/CORBIS, (l) ©Gianni Dagli Orti/CORBIS; **p77** (br) ©Gianni Dagli Orti/CORBIS, (br) Burstein Collection/CORBIS; **p78** ©Gianni Dagli Orti/CORBIS; **p79** (t) The Art Archive/Egyptian Museum Cairo/Dagli Orti, (ml) ©Gianni Dagli Orti/CORBIS; **pp78-79** Art Directors & TRIP/Bob Turner; **p80** (tl, br) ©Gianni Dagli Orti/CORBIS, (ml) Reproduction by permission of the Syndics of The Fitzwilliam Museum, Cambridge; **pp80-81** ©Copyright The British Museum; **p81** The Art Archive/Egyptian Museum Cairo/Dagli Orti; **p82** (tl) ©Michael T. Sedam/CORBIS, (m) ©Copyright The British Museum, (b) ©Gianni Dagli Orti/CORBIS; **p83** ©Gianni Dagli Orti/CORBIS; **p84** (tl, tr) ©Gianni Dagli Orti/CORBIS, (b) Roger Wood/CORBIS; **p85** ©Copyright The British Museum; **p86** (m, wp) ©Copyright The British Museum, (b) ©Wolfgang Kaehler/CORBIS; **p87** (b) ©Werner Forman Archive/CORBIS, (tr, wp) ©Copyright The British Museum; **p88** (tl, l) ©Eye Ubiquitous/CORBIS, (m) ©CORBIS, (b) ©Gianni Dagli Orti/CORBIS; **pp88-89** ©Copyright the British Museum; **p89** ©Gianni Dagli Orti/CORBIS; **p90** (bl & bm) ©Copyright The British Museum, (br) ©Gianni Dagli Orti/CORBIS; **p91** ©Copyright the British Museum; **p94** ©Copyright The British Museum; **p95** (t) ©Eric Crichton/CORBIS, (m) ©Michelle Garrett/CORBIS, (bl) Howard Allman, (tr, br) ©Copyright The British Museum; **pp94-95** ©Peter Johnson/CORBIS; **p96** (tl, bl) ©Gianni Dagli Orti/CORBIS, (ml) ©Copyright The British Museum, (br) ©Papilio/CORBIS; **p97** ©Ludovic Maisant/CORBIS; **pp102-105** ©Gian Berto Vanni/CORBIS; **p107** ©Roger Wood/CORBIS; **p109** ©Gianni Dagli Orti/CORBIS; **pp112-113** ©Historical Picture Archive/CORBIS; **p113** ©Gianni Dagli Orti/CORBIS; **p114** ©Neil Beer/CORBIS; **pp114-115** Popperfoto/Reuters; **p116** (t) With thanks to the Egyptian Museum Cairo, (b) Louvre screenshot ©RMN/Musée du Louvre; **p117** (t) British Museum screenshot ©Copyright The British Museum, (b) Eden Design & Communication ©2001 Rijksmuseum, Amsterdam; **p118** (t) With thanks to the Metropolitan Museum Web site, (b) Museum of Fine Arts screenshot ©Museum of Fine Arts, Boston.